Alzheimer's Survival Guide

ALSO BY
PAUL STANO

The Consumer's Guide
to Hospice Care

The Consumer's Guide
to VA Benefits and
Elder Care Planning

The Funeral Director's Guide
to VA Benefits and
Elder Care Planning

Alzheimer's Survival Guide

7 Secrets of Estate Planning for People with Memory Loss and Dementia

PAUL J. STANO, ESQ.

MITIS·CIVIS
PUBLISHERS
CLEVELAND, OH

THIS MATERIAL IS PRESENTED for informational purposes only. The author has made every attempt to provide the reader with accurate information and makes no claims that using this information will guarantee the reader personal success. While the information contained is about legal issues, it is *not* legal advice.

The discussion of websites, laws, procedures and other information contained in this book is current as of the date of publication. Due to the rapidly changing nature of the law, we recommend a consultation with an Elder Law Attorney prior to initiating any of the steps outlined in this publication. The author shall not be liable for any loss or damage incurred in the process of following advice presented in this book.

Paul J. Stano Co. LPA,
Mitis Civis Publishers, Inc.
Southwest Financial Building
6650 Pearl Road
Parma Hts, OH 44130
Tel: (440) 888.6448

PRINTED IN THE UNITED STATES OF AMERICA

ISBN 978-0-9795864-0-8

FIRST EDITION
13 12 10 09   10 9 8 7 6 5 4

Produced and designed by Randy Martin, martinDESIGN, 44118

NATIONAL ACADEMY OF
ELDER LAW ATTORNEYS

DEDICATION

To
Ann Eakle who died
June 26, 2005,
after a long battle with
Alzheimer's Disease.

And to
Barbara Sue Eakle,
who was her daughter
and loving caregiver
while fighting her own
battle with leukemia.
Barbara joined her mother on
May 10, 2006.

They are gone
but their light still shines.

TABLE OF CONTENTS

INTRODUCTION

ALZHEIMER'S IS A DEGENERATIVE DEMENTIA disease which affects the mind, causing a deterioration in memory, confusion, difficulty with language, severe personality changes and prevents one from doing the most simple tasks. The disease was named for Dr. Alois Alzheimer who discovered it in 1907. Research didn't begin until 1970, however, and to date there is no cure.

There is no way to predict how fast someone will progress through the stages of the disease, but early diagnosis and treatment can slow the progress of the symptoms. There are steps that you can take to manage this disease. Planning for the care of yourself or your loved one will be an emotionally charged subject, but critical to you and your family.

Alzheimer's Survival Guide discusses the stages, symptoms, and problems that manifest themselves in this disease.

Forgetfulness usually comes in the first or second stage of the disease. When you realize that you are forgetting important events, such as a party, a family function, birthdays, your medication or where you parked the car, frustration becomes a reality. Or you may forget to turn off the burner on the stove.

Frustration or annoyance is the second stage.

Frustration gives way to the third stage which is irritability, ill temper and mood swings. Family and friends will have a hard time ignoring these symptoms, but hopefully will be supportive and understanding of the behavior associated with the disease.

Confusion, disorientation and depression follow in the fourth stage of the disease.

Agitation and argumentative attitudes which can show themselves as aggressive behavior complicates things even more in the fifth stage of the disease.

The final stages of the disease may be characterized by hallucinations or disturbed sensory perceptions. Emotional disorders are very often present and active. In the very last stage, you or your loved one may not be able to communicate, speak, eat, swallow, or even get out of bed. The person may become incontinent and may sleep most of the time. Not everyone experiences all the symptoms above, and no two people progress at the same rate through these stages. Keep in mind that outrageous behavior also may be symptoms of over-medication, stimulation from an unknown source, a disproportionate amount of activity, or even a change in daily activity.

One sensitive issue that you should give consideration is who will be your caregiver and his or her role as such. Your caregiver needs to be healthy, strong and in control. The needs of an Alzheimer's patient are greater than with any other affliction or debilitating disease. Your caregiver should have a good relationship with your family and friends, and know how to respond to these challenging changes in your personality.

Alzheimer's Disease raises many questions including medical, legal and financial planning. The *Alzheimer's Survival Guide* cannot address all of them here because each person requires different levels of care, medication, support, financial planning and legal advice. Making these decisions may seem overwhelming for you and your caregiver, especially when everyone is emotionally and physically drained. It is crucial that you involve your doctors, financial planners, and your attorney in your planning as soon as feasible.

As Elder Law Attorneys, we see numerous people suffering from Alzheimer's Disease, dementia, and old age and thus are familiar with the problems facing those involved.

We invite you to contact our office with any questions you may have regarding your specific situation.

Paul J. Stano

Parma Hts., Ohio
June 30, 2007

Alzheimer's Survival Guide

1

EARLY DIAGNOSIS
AND TREATMENT

CONSTANTLY FORGETTING THE NAMES OF
people you know can be embarrassing. It can be
upsetting when you feel anxiety or frustration every
time there is a slight alteration in your daily routine.
Often, it's hard to know whether you are dealing with
Alzheimer's Disease (AD), suffering from high levels
of stress or fatigue, or simply getting older.

If you are becoming increasingly aware of
memory problems or mood swings that are
uncharacteristic, you should consider consulting
your doctor. While it may make you uncomfortable
to discuss these problems, you are not alone.

It's not easy to face the fact that you may be
experiencing early stages of Alzheimer's but it's
extremely important that you find out if you are.

Your doctor may be able to diagnose the cause of
your issues, and offer treatment for the condition so
that the symptoms – all or many – may be reversed.
Unfortunately, in the case of Alzheimer's Disease,

the condition is not reversible. When Alzheimer's is diagnosed early, there are certain things that you can do to better manage the disease.

The Alzheimer's Diagnosis Process

Because no single test can determine whether a person has Alzheimer's, diagnosing someone in the early stages of the disease is often challenging. In recent years, a variety of tests and examinations has allowed doctors to recognize some of the disease's earliest manifestations.

These current assessment practices include:

- A thorough medical history of the patient and their family history;

- An assessment of mental and physical state;

- Psychological assessment and testing;

- A neurological examination and assessment; and

- Lab tests and brain scans.

Although no single test (short of autopsy in which brain tissue can be examined under a microscope) is 100 percent accurate, doctors and specialists are becoming increasingly skilled at analyzing the results of these tests. Most often, they are able to determine the existence or not of Alzheimer's or if the person in question may be suffering from a different issue such as drug reactions or mental or physical disorders.

Current assessment practices help doctors and specialists:

- Identify the cause of symptoms

- Identify any treatable medical conditions or diseases that may or may not be dementia

- Provide a diagnosis

- Provide a base from which a treatment plan can be initiated.

The extent and emphasis of particular tests may be a bit different depending on the specialty of a given doctor or clinician.

Doctors will typically administer the following tests themselves:

- A general physical examination

- Personal medical history

- Blood tests

- Urinalysis

- Imaging tests such as Magnetic Resonance Imaging (MRI) or X-ray

- EEG (Electroencephalogram)

- Lumbar puncture test

- Basic mental status evaluation

Depending on their experience and specialty, the doctor or clinician may then need to refer the patient to a more appropriate specialist. Most commonly, for psychological and neurological tests for Alzheimer's which can include:

- Clinical Interview

- Mini-Mental State Examination (MMSE)

- Clock Drawing Test (CDT)

- Mini-Cog

- Mental Status Examination

- Other Screening and Neurological Tests

Using these methods, doctors are able to make an accurate diagnosis about 90 percent of the time. But memory loss isn't always due to Alzheimer's. It's estimated that 5 to 10 percent of people showing memory loss, confusion and other signs of dementia have a potentially reversible illness, such as metabolic problems, depression, drug intoxication, thyroid problems or vitamin deficiencies. The earlier the diagnosis, generally the easier it is to treat these conditions.

QUALITY OF LIFE IMPROVEMENTS

Although no medications exist that can stop or reverse Alzheimer's, drugs do exist that — if administered early enough — may help treat the symptoms of Alzheimer's. Current treatments aim to improve memory and calm anxieties. Medications and assistive devices can also treat the symptoms of other conditions that may accompany Alzheimer's, including depression, anxiety, infections, or vision and hearing problems.

INCREASED PREPARATION TIME

Early diagnosis gives the patient and the family time to learn about and anticipate changes that accompany the disease, allows early health care and financial decisions (Chapters 2 through 4), or authorizes others to make these decisions when the need arises (Chapters 10 and 11). Early diagnosis also gives you time to modify your home environment and daily routine to accommodate your evolving needs.

Non-medical options and considerations include:

- Becoming familiar with resources available in your area for people with Alzheimer's. Look for options such as support groups, in-home health care aides, adult activity centers and other forms of care.

- Educating yourself about the disease so that you can understand your condition and find creative ways to cope with its symptoms. Talk to your doctor and other health care professionals. Read as much literature on the subject as possible.

- Being open with your family and friends. Discuss plans for future living arrangements and your preferences for medical care and treatment — including end-of-life wishes. Discussing your concerns now will ease the stress for you, your family and friends.

- Asking your doctor for help in telling others about your condition. Print out an article that explains Alzheimer's disease and give it to your friends and family.

- Documenting your wishes by filling out advance directives — special legal papers that let others know what you would like them to do if you can't tell them yourself.

- Appoint someone you trust to handle your financial and legal decisions by giving him or her legal power of attorney. Talk to a lawyer to find out what you need to do to make sure all of your legal and financial documents are in order (Chapters 10 and 11).

- Finding out exactly what your insurance does and doesn't cover in terms of services you may need. Chapter 2 will discuss this in more detail.

- Talking to your employer about arranging a more flexible schedule, if necessary, or look into changing responsibilities.

- Checking around your house to see what changes can easily be made now to provide better accommodations later on. For example, to simplify meal preparation, you may want to purchase and master using a microwave if you've never had one. Learn to use preprogrammed phone numbers so that you don't have to remember complete phone numbers.

- Establishing routines that diminish demands on your memory. Always put your wallet or pocketbook in the same place. Get into the habit of filling and using a weekly pillbox. This way you can check the box if you forget whether you took your pills.

- Keeping your mind active. Playing games, reading, indulging in some creative activities and social interaction are important. Good nutrition and exercise are essential.

Among the most important things for you to remember is that you shouldn't simply give up on your current life-style. Keep up with your hobbies, family, friends and interests. If you stop working, pick up a new hobby or try volunteer work.

You're Not Alone: Get Support

Even though news of the diagnosis may seem frightening, remember that you aren't alone. More than 4 million people in the United States have Alzheimer's disease. It may help to talk with other people who have similar experiences and who are coping with the disease.

Many communities have support groups for people with Alzheimer's and their loved ones. A support group can become an important place to find practical information, solve problems, share stories and discover new ways to cope with the disease.

Specific support groups exist for caregivers, for those with early-onset Alzheimer's, and for families of people with Alzheimer's. For information about support groups near you, contact your local chapter of the Alzheimer's Association or call the national office at 800-272-3900.

What If You Think Someone You Know May Have Alzheimer's?

Approaching someone you know and love about your suspicions that they may have Alzheimer's isn't an easy thing to do. If you do think that this may be the cause of some of the symptoms you've witnessed in someone you know, it is important that you bring it to light as soon as you can, so that they can seek diagnosis early.

Remember, they may not even be aware of some of the more subtle symptoms, or they may be aware of them and be brushing them off in the hope that they'll go away or be caused by something else.

Keep in mind that many of the symptoms produced by Alzheimer's can be attributed to a number of other issues, including chronic stress, depression, drug interactions, and other disorders. These may be easily treatable, so it is still important that they be recognized as early as possible.

Either way, early recognition is the key, so that the person you know and love can appreciate the best quality of life, and make all of the necessary arrangements to know that everything will be taken care of.

It may be a difficult thing to do, but if you approach your friend or family member with compassion, caring, and love, they'll know that you have their best interests in mind, and the next step —diagnosis — can be made.

●

I WAS ALWAYS TAUGHT TO RESPECT MY ELDERS AND I'VE NOW REACHED THE AGE WHEN I DON'T HAVE ANYBODY TO RESPECT.
— GEORGE BURNS

2

LONG TERM CARE
INSURANCE

DUE TO THE SLOW, PROGRESSIVE NATURE
of Alzheimer's Disease, it can be extremely costly to
care for a loved one. Studies have shown that on
average, the cost of caring for an Alzheimer's patient
can be $200,000 or more. Few people can afford this
level of expense. Fortunately, there are places you can
turn for help. Long-term care insurance is an option
and a very sound strategy. It is a complex product
and offers several forms of protection.

What is Long-Term Care?
Insurance is an important tool for protecting
yourself against risk. For instance, health insurance
pays your doctor and hospital bills if you get sick or
injured. But how can you protect yourself against the
significant financial risk posed by the potential need
for long-term care services, whether at home, with
community services, in an assisted living facility, or
in a nursing home?

Adequate care for Alzheimer's Disease is more than medical and nursing. It must include all the assistance you would need should you become unable to care for yourself for an extended period of time and may include services such as:
• Visiting nurse
• Home health aides
• Friendly visitor programs
• Home delivered meals
• Chore services
• Adult day care centers
• Respite services for caregivers who need a break from daily responsibilities

These services are widely available and some or all of them may be found in your community. Your local Area Agency on Aging or Office on Aging can help you locate the services you need.

Without Long-Term Insurance, paying for them will require the use of savings or assets.

WHAT DOES LONG-TERM CARE COST?
Long-term care can be very expensive and the real amount you will spend depends on the level of services you need and the length of time you need care. One year in a nursing home can average more than $60,000. In some regions, it can easily cost twice that amount.

The average monthly fee assisted living facilities charge is around $4,000. This includes rent and most additional fees. Some residents in the facility may pay significantly more if their care needs are higher.

Home care is less expensive but is still costly. Bringing an aide into your home just three times a week (two to three hours per visit) to help with dressing, bathing, preparing meals and similar household chores can easily cost $1,000 each month, or $12,000 a year. Add in the cost of skilled help, such as physical therapists, and these costs can be much greater.

WHO PAYS THE BILLS?

For the most part, the Alzheimer's sufferer is the one required to pay the bills. Individuals and their families pay about one-fourth of all nursing home costs out-of-pocket. Generally, long-term care isn't covered by the health insurance you may have either on your own or through your employer.

What about the government? Generally, Medicare will not cover long-term care beyond the first 99 days. People over 65 and some younger people with disabilities have health coverage through the federal Medicare program. Medicare pays for short-term skilled nursing home care following hospitalization. Medicare also pays for some skilled at-home care, but only for short-term unstable medical conditions and not for the ongoing assistance that many elderly, ill, or injured people need.

Medicare supplement insurance (often called Medigap or MedSupp) is private insurance that helps cover some of the gaps in Medicare coverage. While these policies help pay the deductible for hospitals and doctors, coinsurance payments, or what Medicare considers excess physician charges, they do not cover long-term care.

Medicaid — the federal program that provides custodial health care coverage — pays almost half of all nursing home costs. Medicaid pays benefits either immediately, for people meeting Federal guidelines, or after nursing home residents exhaust their savings and become eligible. Turning to Medicaid once meant impoverishing the spouse who remained at home as well as the spouse confined to a nursing home. However, the law permits the at-home spouse to retain specified levels of assets and income. Medicaid will be discussed in greater detail in Chapter 6.

It's impossible to predict precisely what kind of care you might need in the future, or know exactly what the costs will be, since the progression of Alzheimer's is different for each person. However, like other insurance, long-term care insurance allows people to pay a known premium for a policy to protect against the risk of much larger out-of-pocket expenses.

Since it is, however, likely you will need long-term care at one point or another throughout the progression of the Alzheimer's disease, you should learn about the appropriate insurance coverage available for your needs.

WHERE CAN I GET LONG-TERM CARE COVERAGE?

Long-term care insurance is sold privately through insurance companies. Although long-term care insurance is relatively new, more than 100 companies now offer coverage.

Long-term care insurance is generally available through groups and to individuals. Group insurance is typically offered through employers, and this type of coverage is becoming a more common benefit. By the end of 2002, more than 5,600 employers were offering a long-term care insurance plan to their employees, retirees, or both.

Individual long-term care insurance coverage is a good option if you are not employed, if you work for a small company that doesn't offer a plan, or if you are self-employed. If you are retired or elderly, you should consider long-term care insurance as a resource to protect yourself and your loved one against rising health care costs.

Choosing a policy requires careful shopping because coverage and costs vary from company to company and depend on the benefit levels you choose.

WHAT ARE THE TYPES OF LONG-TERM CARE POLICIES? Several types of policies are available. Most are known as *indemnity* or *expense incurred* policies.

An indemnity or *per diem* policy pays up to a fixed benefit amount regardless of what you spend. With an expense-incurred policy, you choose the benefit amount when you buy the policy and you are reimbursed for actual expenses for services received up to a fixed dollar amount per day, week, or month.

Today, many companies also offer *integrated policies* or policies with *pooled benefits*. This type of policy provides a total dollar amount that may be used for different types of long-term care services. There is usually a daily, weekly, or monthly dollar limit for your covered long-term care expenses.

For example, say you purchase a policy with a maximum benefit amount of $150,000 of pooled benefits. Under this policy, you would have a daily benefit of $150 that would last for 1,000 days if you spend the maximum daily amount on care. If, however, your care costs less, you would receive benefits for more than 1,000 days.

There are no policies that guarantee to cover all expenses fully.

You usually have a choice of daily benefit amounts ranging from $50 to more than $300 per day for nursing home coverage. The daily benefit for at-home care may be less than the benefit for nursing home care. It's important to keep in mind that you are responsible for your actual nursing home or home care costs that exceed the daily benefit amount you purchased.

Because the per day benefit you buy today may not be enough to cover higher costs years from now, most policies offer inflation adjustments. In many policies, for example, the initial benefit amount will increase automatically each year at a specified rate (such as 5 percent) compounded over the life of the policy.

Some life insurance policies offer long-term care benefits. With these accelerated or living benefits provisions, under certain circumstances a portion of the life insurance benefit is paid to the policyholder for long-term care services instead of to the beneficiary at the policyholder's death. Some companies make these benefits available to all policyholders; others offer them only to people buying new policies.

What Do Policies Cost?

The cost of long-term care insurance varies widely, depending on the options you choose. For example, inflation adjustments can increase your premium by 40 to 100 percent. However, this option can keep benefits in line with the current cost of care.

The actual premium you will pay depends on many factors, including your age, the level of benefits, and the length of time you are willing to wait until benefits begin. A licensed long-term care insurance agent or a financial advisor can help in balancing policy features and premium cost.

There are several creative options to pay for long-term care insurance such as employee stock ownership plans (ESOPs), pensions, paid-up life insurance or a single premium annuity, or, of course, your savings. Talk with a financial planner, insurance agent or your attorney before making any decisions.

Age

In 2002, a policy offering a $150 per day long-term care benefit for four years, with a 90-day deductible, cost a 50 year old a national average of $564 per year. For someone who was 65 years old, the national average cost was $1,337, and for a 79 year old, the national average cost was $5,330. The same policy with an inflation protection feature cost, on average nationally, $1,134 at age 50, $2,346 at age 65, and $7,572 at age 79. Please note that these are only national averages. The cost of long-term care varies significantly by state. For the cost of care and coverage in your area, check with a representative of a long-term care insurer, an insurance agent, or financial adviser. Additionally, the younger you are when you first buy a policy, the lower your annual premium will be.

BENEFITS

The amount of your premium also depends on the amount of the daily benefit and how long you wish that benefit to be paid. For example, a policy that pays $100 a day for up to five years of long-term care costs more than a policy that pays $50 a day for three years.

ELIMINATION OR DEDUCTIBLE PERIODS

Elimination or deductible periods are the number of days you must be in residence at a nursing home or the number of home care visits you must receive before policy benefits begin. For instance, with a 20 day elimination period your policy will begin paying benefits on the twenty-first day. Most policies offer a choice of deductible ranging from zero to 180 days. The longer the elimination or deductible period, the lower the premium will be.

However, longer elimination periods also mean higher out-of-pocket costs. For instance, if you have a policy with a 100 day waiting period and you go to a nursing home for a year, you must pay for 100 days of care. If your stay costs $150 a day, your total cost would be $15,000. With a 30-day elimination period, your cost would be only $4,500.

When you're considering a long-term care policy, you should determine not just how much you can pay for premiums but also how long you could pay for your own care. Bear in mind that while 45 percent of nursing home stays last three months or less, more than one-third last one year or longer. The more costly longer stay may be the devastating financial blow that you may want to insure against.

WILL MY PREMIUMS INCREASE AS I GET OLDER?

In general, premiums will stay the same each year. If they do increase, it will be for the whole class of policyholders, not because you as an individual have aged, your health has deteriorated, or your Alzheimer's Disease has progressed.

WHAT DO LONG-TERM CARE INSURANCE POLICIES COVER?

Long-term care services are provided when a person cannot perform certain "activities of daily living" (ADLs), or is cognitively impaired because of senile dementia or Alzheimer's disease. Most commonly, the ADLs used to determine the need for services include bathing, dressing, transferring (getting from a bed to a chair), toileting, eating, and continence. Instrumental Activities of Daily Living (IADLs) include such activities as preparing meals, shopping, managing money, housework, taking medications, and the ability to use the telephone. Most policies pay benefits only when one becomes incapacitated that he can no longer physically or mentally take care of his own basic needs or requires help in dressing, feeding or needs supervision because of disorientation.

Today's policies cover skilled, intermediate, and custodial care in state-licensed nursing homes. Long-term care policies usually also cover home care services such as skilled or non-skilled nursing care, physical therapy, homemakers, and home health aides provided by state-licensed and/or Medicare-certified home health agencies.

Many policies also cover assisted living, adult day care, other care in the community, alternate care, and respite care for the caregiver.

Alternate care is non-conventional care and services developed by a licensed health care practitioner that serves as an alternative to more costly nursing home care. Benefits for alternate care may be available for special medical care and treatments, different sites of care, or medically necessary modifications to the insured's home, like building ramps for wheelchairs or modifications to a kitchen or bathroom. A health care professional develops the alternate plan of care, the insured or insurer may initiate the plan and the insurer approves it.

You should know that the benefit amount paid for alternate care will reduce the maximum or lifetime benefit available for later confinement in a long-term care facility. Policies may limit the expenses covered under this benefit (for instance, 60 percent of the lifetime maximum limit).

Alzheimer's disease and other organic cognitive disabilities are leading causes for nursing home admissions and worry for many older Americans. These conditions are generally covered under long-term care policies.

What is not Covered?

All policies contain limits and exclusions to keep premiums reasonable and affordable. These are likely to differ from policy to policy. Before you buy, be sure you understand exactly what is and is not covered under a particular policy.

Preexisting Conditions

Preexisting conditions are health problems you had when you became insured. Insurance companies may require that a period of time pass before the policy pays for care related to these conditions. For example, a company may exclude coverage of preexisting conditions for six months. This means that if you need long-term care within six months of the policy's issue date for that condition, you may be denied benefits. Companies do not generally exclude coverage for preexisting conditions for more than six months.

Specific Exclusions

Some mental and nervous disorders are not covered. Alcoholism, drug abuse, and an intentionally self-inflicted injury usually are not covered.

What Else Should I Know Before I Buy?

Virtually all policies now cover Alzheimer's disease and no longer require a hospital stay before paying nursing home benefits. Different options are available under different policies. These are:

ELIGIBILITY

If you are in reasonably good health, can take care of yourself, and are between the ages of 18 and 84, you can probably buy long-term care insurance. Some companies do not sell individual policies to people under age 18 or over age 84. Age limitations apply only to your age at the time of purchase, not at the time you use the benefits.

DURATION OR DOLLAR LIMITATIONS OF BENEFITS

Long-term care policies generally limit benefits to a maximum dollar amount or a maximum number of days and may have separate benefit limits for nursing home, assisted living facility, and home health care within the same policy. For example, a policy may offer $100 per day up to five years of nursing home coverage (many policies now offer lifetime nursing home coverage) and only up to $80 per day up to five years of assisted living and home health care coverage.

Generally, there are two ways a company defines a policy's maximum benefit period. Under one definition, a policy may offer a one-time maximum benefit period. A policy with five years of nursing home coverage, issued by a company using this definition, would pay only for a total of five years in a policyholder's lifetime.

Other policies offer a maximum benefit period for each "period of disability." A policy with a five year maximum benefit period would cover more than one nursing home stay lasting up to five years each if the periods of disability were separated by six months or more.

ABILITY TO RENEW

Virtually all long-term care policies sold to individuals are guaranteed renewable; they cannot be canceled as long as you pay your premiums on time and as long as you have told the truth about your health on the application. Premiums can be increased, however, if they are increased for an entire group of policyholders.

The renewability provision, normally found on the first page of the policy, specifies under what conditions the policy can be canceled and when premiums may increase.

NON-FORFEITURE BENEFITS

This benefit returns to policyholders some of their benefits if they drop their coverage. Most companies now offer this option. The most common types of non-forfeiture benefits offered today are *return of premium* or a *shortened benefit period.*

With a return of premium benefit, the policyholder receives cash, usually a percent of the total premiums paid to date after lapse or death. With a shortened benefit period, the long-term care coverage continues, but the benefit period or duration amount is reduced as specified in the policy. A non-forfeiture benefit can add from 20 to 100 percent to a policy's cost.

Some policies may offer "contingent non-forfeiture benefits upon lapse," a feature that gives policyholders additional options in the face of a significant increase in policy premiums. If you do not purchase the optional non-forfeiture benefit, then a contingent non-forfeiture benefit is triggered if policy premiums rise by a specified percentage. For example, if at age 70 your premium rises to 40 percent above the original premium, you have the option of either decreasing the amount your policy pays per day of care or of converting to a policy with a shorter duration of benefits.

WAIVER OF PREMIUM

This provision allows you to stop paying premiums during the time you are receiving benefits. Read the policy carefully to see if there are any restrictions on this provision, such as a requirement to be in a nursing home for any length of time (90 days is a typical requirement) or receiving home health care before premiums are waived.

DISCLOSURE

Your medical history is very important because the insurance company uses the information you provide on your application to assess your eligibility for coverage. The application must be accurate and complete. If it is not, the insurance company may be within its rights to deny coverage when you file a claim. In fact, many companies now waive the preexisting condition requirement if you fully disclose your medical history and are issued a policy.

What About Switching Policies?

New long-term care insurance policies may have more favorable provisions than older policies. Newer policies, for instance, generally do not require prior hospital stays or certain levels of care before benefits begin. But, if you do switch, preexisting condition exclusions for specified periods of time will have to begin again. In addition, your new premiums may be higher because they will be based on your current age.

You should never switch policies before making sure the new policy is better than the one you already have. And you should never drop an old policy before making sure the new one is in force.

What Should I Look for in a Policy?

The National Association of Insurance Commissioners has developed standards that protect consumers. You should look for a policy that includes:

- At least one year of nursing home or home health care coverage, including intermediate and custodial care. Nursing home or home health care benefits should not be limited primarily to skilled care.

- Coverage for Alzheimer's disease, should the policyholder develop it after purchasing the policy.

- An inflation protection option. The policy should offer a choice among:

- automatically increasing the initial benefit level on an annual basis,
- a guaranteed right to increase benefit levels periodically without providing evidence of insurability.
- An *outline of coverage* that systematically describes the policy's benefits, limitations, and exclusions and also allows you to compare it with others.

- A long-term care insurance shopper's guide that helps you decide whether long-term care insurance is appropriate for you. Your company or agent should provide both of these.

- A guarantee that the policy cannot be canceled, non-renewed, or otherwise terminated because you get older or suffer deterioration in physical or mental health.

- The right to return the policy within 30 days after you have purchased the policy and to receive a premium refund.

- No requirement that policyholders:
    - first be hospitalized in order to receive nursing home benefits or home health care benefits,
    - first receive skilled nursing home care before receiving intermediate or custodial nursing home care,
    - first receive nursing home care before receiving benefits for home health care.

Before You Buy

Insurance policies are legal contracts. Read and compare the policies you are considering before you buy one. Make sure you understand all of the provisions. Marketing or sales literature is no substitute for the actual policy. Read the policy itself before you buy.

Discuss the policies you are considering with people whose opinions you respect—perhaps your doctor, financial advisor, your children, or an informed friend or relative.

Ask for the insurance company's financial rating and for a summary of each policy's benefits or an outline of coverage. (Ratings result from analyses of a company's financial records.) Good agents and good insurance companies want you to know what you are buying.

And bear in mind: Even after you buy a policy, if you find that it does not meet your needs you generally have 30 days to return the policy and get your money back. This is called the "free look" period.

Do not give in to high pressure sales tactics. Do not be afraid to ask your insurance agent to explain anything that is unclear. If you are not satisfied with an agent's answers, ask for someone to contact in the company itself. Call your state insurance department if you are not satisfied with the answers you get from the agent or from company representatives.

LONG-TERM CARE POLICY CHECKLIST

Before you begin shopping, you should find out how much nursing home or home health care costs in your area today. If you needed care right away, could you find it locally or would you have to go to another potentially more expensive area?

Once you've done some research, you can use the following checklist to help you compare policies you may be considering.

- What services are covered?
  - Nursing home care
  - Home health care
  - Assisted living facility
  - Adult day care
  - Alternate care
  - Respite care
  - Other

- How much does the policy pay per day for nursing home care? For home health care? For an assisted living facility? For adult day care? For alternate care? For respite care? Other?

- How long will benefits last in a nursing home? At home? In an assisted living facility? Other?

- Does the policy have a maximum lifetime benefit? If so, what is it for nursing home care? For home health care? For an assisted living facility? Other?

- Does the policy have a maximum length of coverage for each period of confinement? If so, what is it for nursing home care? For home health care? For an assisted living facility?

- How long must I wait before preexisting conditions are covered?

- How many days must I wait before benefits begin for nursing home care? For home health care? For an assisted living facility? Other?

- Are Alzheimer's disease and other organic mental and nervous disorders covered?

- Does this policy require:
    - An assessment of activities of daily living?
    - An assessment of cognitive impairment?
    - Physician certification of need?
    - A prior hospital stay for nursing home care or home health care?
    - A prior nursing home stay for home health care coverage? Other?

- Is the policy guaranteed renewable?

- What is the age range for enrollment?

- Is there a waiver-of-premium provision for nursing home care? For home health care?

- How long must I be confined before premiums are waived?

- Does the policy have a non-forfeiture benefit?

- Does the policy offer an inflation adjustment feature? If so, what is the rate of increase? How often is it applied? For how long? Is there an additional cost?

- What does the policy cost...
  - Per year?
  - With inflation feature?
  - Without inflation feature?
  - With non-forfeiture feature?
  - Without non-forfeiture feature?
  - Per month?
  - With inflation feature?
  - Without inflation feature?
  - With non-forfeiture feature?
  - Without non-forfeiture feature?

- Is there a 30-day free look?

HIPAA'S IMPACT ON LONG-TERM CARE INSURANCE

The Health Insurance Portability and Accountability Act of 1996 (HIPAA) affects how premiums and benefits are taxed and offers consumer protection standards for long-term care insurance. The following are answers to commonly asked questions about HIPAA:

TAX TREATMENT

You should familiarize yourself with the following list of issues regarding the tax treatment accompanying long-term care insurance.

- Tax clarifications for private long-term care insurance assure that, like major medical coverage, benefits from qualified long-term care insurance plans generally are not taxed. Without HIPAA clarifications, these benefits might be considered taxable income.

- Consumers are able to take a tax deduction for the premiums they pay on a tax-qualified long-term care insurance policy. Consumers may also deduct from their taxes costs associated with receiving long-term care. HIPAA says that qualified long-term care insurance will now receive the same tax treatment as accident and health insurance. That means that premiums for long-term care insurance, as well as consumers' out-of-pocket expenses for long-term care, can be applied toward meeting the federal tax codes' 7.5 percent floor for medical expense deductions. However, there are limits, based on a policyholder's age, for the total amount of long-term care premiums that can be applied toward the 7.5 percent minimum. (Check with your financial planner or tax adviser to see if you are eligible to take this deduction.)

- Generally, employers are able to deduct as a business expense both the cost of setting up a long-term care insurance plan for their employees and the contributions that they may make toward paying for the cost of premiums.

- Will employer contributions be excluded from the taxable income of employees?

- Individual Retirement Accounts (IRAs) and 401(k) funds may not be used to purchase private long-term care insurance. However, under a demonstration project, tax-free funds deposited in Medical Savings Accounts can be used to pay long-term care insurance premiums.

CONSUMER PROTECTION STANDARDS

Along with taxation knowledge, you should also know your rights regarding protection standards and tax treatment with long-term care plans.

The following are some interesting points to be considered:

- To qualify for favorable tax treatment, a long-term care policy sold after 1996 must contain the consumer protection standards in HIPAA. Also, insurance companies must follow certain administrative and marketing practices or face significant fines. Policies sold prior to January 1, 1997, automatically will be eligible for favorable tax treatment. Lastly, nothing in the new law prevents states from imposing more stringent consumer protection standards.

- There are several kinds of consumer protections insurance companies employ to meet HIPAA standards. Consumers must receive a *Shopper's Guide* and a description of the policy's benefits and limitations (i.e., Outline of Coverage) early in the sales process. The Outline of Coverage allows consumers to compare policies from different companies. Companies must report annually the number of claims denied and information on policy replacement sales and policy terminations. Sales practices such as *twisting* — knowingly making misleading or incomplete comparisons of policies — are prohibited, as are high-pressure sales tactics.

- HIPAA standards address limits on benefits and exclusions from coverage. According to HIPAA, no policy can be sold as a long-term care insurance policy if it limits or excludes coverage by type of treatment, medical condition, or accident. However, there are several exceptions to this rule. For example, policies may limit or exclude coverage for preexisting conditions or diseases, mental or nervous disorders (but not Alzheimer's), or alcoholism or drug addiction. A policy cannot, however, exclude coverage for preexisting conditions for more than six months after the effective date of coverage.

- The law prohibits a company from canceling a policy except for nonpayment of premiums. Policies cannot be canceled because of age or deterioration of mental or physical health. In fact, if a policyholder is late paying a premium, the policy can be reinstated up to five months later if the reason for nonpayment is shown to be cognitive impairment.

- These standards will help people who, for whatever reason, lose their group coverage. People covered by a group policy will be allowed to continue their coverage when they leave their employer, so long as they pay their premiums in a timely fashion. Further, an individual who has been covered under a group plan for at least six months may convert to an individual policy if and when the group plan is discontinued. The individual may do so without providing evidence of insurability.

If You Need Help

Every state has a Department of Insurance that regulates insurers and assists consumers. If you need more information, or if you want to register a complaint, check the government listings in your local phone book for your State's Department of Insurance.

Additional information about long-term care coverage is available from the Area Agency on Aging.

Other sources include:

• American Health Care Association
  1201 L Street, N.W.
  Washington, D.C. 20005
  (202) 842-4444
  www.ahca.org

• National Council on the Aging
  300 D Street, SW, Suite 801
  Washington, DC 20024
  (202) 479-1200
  www.ncoa.org

•

IT IS A MISTAKE TO REGARD AGE
AS A DOWNHILL GRADE TOWARD
DISSOLUTION. THE REVERSE IS
TRUE. AS ONE GROWS OLDER,
ONE CLIMBS WITH SURPRISING
STRIDES.
— GEORGE SAND

3

REVERSE MORTGAGES

REVERSE MORTGAGES ARE BECOMING A popular method to obtain the funding required throughout the progression of Alzheimer's Disease because they offer senior homeowners a way to turn their home equity into cash, tax free. To qualify:

- You must own your home

- You must be at least 62 years of age

- Your home must be your principle place of residence.

WHAT IS A REVERSE MORTGAGE?
In a reverse (or conversion) mortgage, the home is used as collateral to get tax-free cash from the equity of the home without incurring monthly expenses. With a reverse mortgage, the homeowner does not need an income to qualify.

How Do Reverse Mortgages Work?

The amount of a reverse mortgage is determined by the age of the home, the current interest rate, and the home's value. The homeowners can pull needed cash from the equity of the home without incurring monthly expenses. The homeowner can receive payments in a lump sum or on a monthly basis for as long as they live in their home.

Once the property is sold — and this can be during the homeowner's lifetime or after his or her death — the sale price of the property pays back the loan and the interest. This rule is in place *even if the sale price is less than the combination of the loan and interest*.

Lenders must accept *only* the sale price and cannot by law go after the homeowner's other assets.

What are the Advantages of a Reverse Mortgage?

Lenders cannot force homeowners to sell the property to pay back the loan. Reverse mortgages guarantee that the homeowner can stay on the property for as long as he or she lives, *even if the outstanding loan and interest grow to exceed the property's value.*

Only you can decide what a reverse mortgage is worth to you.

A reverse mortgage can be a sound strategy to:

- Increase your income

- Pay unexpected expenses

- Pay off debts

- Make necessary changes to your home

- Make your home more accessible

- Help you get the home care services you need to remain independent.

Reverse mortgages can be used for:

- Medical bills and prescription drugs

- Long-term health care

- Retirement and estate tax planning

- Daily living expenses.

Another important consideration is that any remaining value on the home goes to the homeowner or his heirs when the house is sold.

WHAT ARE THE DISADVANTAGES OF A REVERSE MORTGAGE?

The costs associated with a Reverse Mortgage are very similar to those of a conventional loan:

- Origination fees

- Inspection fees

- Appraisal and title fees

- Mortgage insurance

- Normal closing costs

- Monthly servicing fees.

Reverse mortgage fees can be high, although fees are usually rolled into the loan and not paid up front. A reverse mortgage can cost thousands more than a conventional mortgage. One lower cost option is the FHA reverse mortgage program from the U.S. Department of Housing & Urban Development (HUD).

All reverse mortgages carry adjustable interest rates. Some programs give you the option to choose a rate that adjusts annually or monthly. Annual rate adjustments may offer a lower loan amount but are usually capped at two points per year or five points over the life of the loan. Monthly rate adjustments may offer a larger loan amount, but they usually have no annual cap, and instead are capped at ten points over the life of the loan. If you choose to receive your reverse mortgage funds as monthly cash payments, these rate adjustments will not change the amount you receive each month. They only affect the amount of interest that is charged on the total loan balance.

It's important to calculate the cost of a reverse mortgage against what you would gain, because once you enter a reverse mortgage agreement, the mortgage company may end up with all the equity in the property.

Having a reverse mortgage may offer the ability to take advantage of planning options that require monthly payments which otherwise might not be available to an older homeowner.

Be sure that the older homeowner is thinking clearly when considering a reverse mortgage. The prospect of a sudden influx of cash can make it seem as though all their problems will be solved.

Because there are many things to consider, including the possibility of lenders who do not have the homeowner's best interests in mind, it is imperative to get sound advice. Discuss your reverse mortgage plans with your legal and financial advisors and family members before making a decision.

Home ownership is often a person's most valuable asset. It's important to remember that getting a reverse mortgage is essentially the same as withdrawing the money you'd expect to leave to your heirs.

What are the Rules of Reverse Mortgages?
To reduce their risk, lenders generally limit reverse mortgage loans to amounts that are below their estimate of the property's full value.

Age is an advantage when applying for a reverse mortgage. Borrowers must be at least age 62. The older the homeowner is, the more money he or she would qualify for. For example, a 78 year old borrower would qualify for a larger loan than a 62 year old.

What are the Limits on Reverse Mortgages?

Limits can vary across the country. The most popular option, the Home Equity Conversion Mortgage, which accounts for nine of every 10 reverse mortgages in the U.S., limits loans to $312,896.

The Fannie Mae Home Keeper loan, number two in popularity, limits loan amounts to $359,650.

Using Reverse Mortgages to Fund Long-Term Care

No person should have to sacrifice his or her home or an opportunity for independence to secure necessary health care and supportive services.

Most elders who need long-term care would prefer to stay in their own homes. A 2000 consumer survey found that over 90 percent of people 65 and older strongly or somewhat agree that they wish to remain in their homes as long as possible. With today's innovative technology and in-home services, this is increasingly possible.

Even severely impaired elders can now continue to live at home if they receive appropriate assistance. Without adequate financial support, however, even modest costs for home care can be prohibitive to many older Americans. The cost of help at home for physically or mentally impaired elders can range dramatically, from an average of $200 per month in out-of-pocket expenses by family caregivers to more than $6,000 per month for elders who need round-the-clock care from home-care professionals.

One way to assess the value of a reverse mortgage for long-term care is to determine the planning options available with the proceeds from the mortgage. Because reverse mortgages have relatively high closing costs, this financial tool offers a better value for people who expect to live at home for more than five years. It can be an expensive choice for borrowers who opt for a lump sum and then move out, sell their home, or happen to die within a few years of taking out the loan.

Currently, the reverse mortgage loan becomes due if the last remaining borrower requires care in a nursing home or assisted living facility for more than a year. For severely impaired elders who take out a reverse mortgage, there is a risk that they will not be able to remain at home for many years.

A lump-sum payment will be most helpful for borrowers, who can use these funds immediately to make major home modifications, pay for a high level of home-care services, or utilize estate planning options requiring cash. Borrowers who live alone and lack informal caregivers, may also benefit from having a large sum available to pay for professional help at home or to fund their retirement plans (if they have a spouse in a nursing home).

By liquidating their housing wealth through a reverse mortgage, elder homeowners, especially those who are "house rich and cash poor," could access a significant amount of cash to pay for long-term care. For example, households who are dealing with Alzheimer's disease limitations could convert a home they own free and clear worth $150,000 into a loan ranging in value from about $60,000 to $100,000, depending on the age of the youngest homeowner.

These amounts will fund a significant amount of paid home care to help impaired seniors avoid or delay the need for institutionalization. For example, the average home health aid charges about $72 per visit. Adult day care services cost about $50 per day. At these rates, a 75 year-old borrower with Alzheimer's impairments would be able to receive daily home care visits for almost three years.

Borrowers who are less impaired, or who can get some help from family or friends, could significantly increase the amount of time that they might be able to continue to live at home. For example, elders who require only three days of paid home care per week would be able to use their loan to pay for assistance for more than five years.

Many Alzheimer's sufferers find that the need for long-term care arises slowly, as they gradually require more help with everyday activities at home. For these elders, it may be more appropriate to receive payments from a reverse mortgage through a credit line or tenure payment (which pays for as long as the borrower lives in the home). In fact, most reverse mortgage borrowers elect to receive their payments through a line of credit, either alone (68 percent) or in combination with a tenure or term payment plan (20 percent).

ESTIMATED DURATION OF FUNDS

A borrower, age 75, could withdraw from a reverse mortgage line of credit each month. Since Alzheimer's patients who live at home may need assistance for a long time, these amounts can be deducted from a credit line that would last for approximately three to 10 years. The amounts that would be available monthly to "impaired" households vary depending on the value of the home.

These funds could have a significant impact on the finances of Alzheimer's patients and their families. By having money of their own to pay for long-term care, elders can maintain their dignity, as well as retain some independence and control over their lives. For spouses and other family caregivers, these supports can help reduce the financial, emotional and physical strain that often comes with caring for an impaired elder.

Reverse Mortgages and Long-Term Care Insurance

Keep in mind that with financing, long-term care is a risk, not a certainty. Since this is the case, most experts recommend that long-term Alzheimer's care should be insured against, not saved for.

The equity that most Alzheimer's patients have accumulated in their home would not be sufficient to pay the entire cost of the long-term Alzheimer's care they will require if they require increased levels of assistance, or assistance for a long time.

It must also be considered that these funds may also be inadequate to meet the needs of couples if both spouses became severely impaired. To shield homeowners from potentially catastrophic costs of long-term care, they will need additional resources. One important option is long-term care insurance.

Reverse mortgages could significantly increase the affordability of long-term care insurance. By tapping home equity, homeowners can purchase a policy without having to sacrifice their current lifestyle. There are several options to increase the affordability of long-term care insurance using funds from a reverse mortgage.

One strategy uses the proceeds of a reverse mortgage to pay for insurance premiums. Another approach would limit the amount of insurance purchased by elders by increasing the amount of long-term care self-funded through a reverse mortgage.

Using a reverse mortgage to pay for long-term care insurance premiums could save current cash assets for other uses.

These three criteria must be met in order to consider a reverse mortgage as a source of funds for long-term care insurance:

1. Reverse mortgage borrowers should have *insurability* to purchase a meaningful amount of long-term care coverage.

2. Payments from a reverse mortgage should pay for a substantial proportion of the insurance premiums, and for any future premium increases. This would be particularly important for *house rich and cash poor* elders who have few other resources with which to pay for coverage.

3. Reverse mortgage proceeds must last long enough to pay premiums until a policyholder needs long-term care. Otherwise, a policyholder is at risk of lapsing their coverage without getting any benefits from the insurance.

Each of these criteria raises important issues that need to be addressed about the potential market for this approach and the cost versus value of the benefit to borrowers.

It is difficult to determine how much long-term care coverage a person should purchase. Elders with Alzheimer's disease commonly need assistance lasting six years or longer.

Both single individuals and couples who own homes worth at least $100,000 would be able to use the proceeds of a reverse mortgage to buy a five year policy. Singles with a home worth $100,000 and couples with housing wealth of about $150,000 could also afford lifetime coverage.

However, using most of the proceeds from a reverse mortgage to pay for long-term care coverage might be risky for many households. After paying for insurance premiums, they would have little left from their monthly reverse mortgage cash withdrawal to pay for expenses not covered by the $150 per day long-term care benefit or for any premium increases. Since private insurance only pays when policyholders are severely impaired, these homeowners could also face financial problems if they needed help to stay at home prior to triggering their insurance benefits.

For elders with modest amounts of housing wealth, using reverse mortgages for long-term care insurance is not likely to be an option. Single homeowners, age 70, with a home worth $50,000, who use the entire monthly withdrawal from their reverse mortgage line of credit for long-term care insurance, would be able to pay about 80 percent of the cost of premiums.

For couples in this group, cash withdrawals from a reverse mortgage would cover the cost of about 50 percent of their policy premiums.

Duration of the loan is a critical factor in linking reverse mortgages and private insurance. The risk of needing long-term care increases significantly after age 85. For the typical reverse mortgage borrower who takes out a loan in his 70s, this could mean holding onto the loan for five to 15 years or longer. Because the reverse mortgage program is relatively new, even experts do not yet have a good understanding of how long reverse mortgage borrowers keep their loans.

Preliminary evidence, however, suggests that reverse mortgage borrowers are repaying their loans at a faster rate than would be expected from mortality and move-out rates among older homeowners in general. Further research will be needed to determine the reasons why borrowers terminate their loans and the potential impact this could have on funding long-term care insurance.

Congress passed a provision within the American Homeownership and Economic Opportunity Act of 2000 that encourages the use of reverse mortgages for the purchase of long-term care insurance. Under this new law, HUD is authorized to waive the up-front mortgage insurance premium for reverse mortgage borrowers who use all the proceeds of their reverse mortgage to purchase a tax-qualified long-term care insurance policy.

An analysis of the new law suggests that there is likely to be low demand for this financing option. This is primarily due to the lack of overlap in the economic and demographic characteristics of typical reverse mortgage borrowers and long-term care insurance buyers. Implementing this new reverse mortgage provision could also present many challenges to HUD. For example, it would be difficult to track whether borrowers are using all the proceeds of their loan to pay for private long-term care insurance.

Use of home equity, particularly through a reverse mortgage, can be an important retirement resource to help impaired elders pay for long-term care services in the home and community. Due to the widespread availability of home equity, using reverse mortgages is an inclusive strategy that strengthens the long-term care safety net for all elders. This is especially important for moderate income elders whose financial needs in retirement often go unaddressed.

Funds from reverse mortgages are available in several payment plans and can be used without restrictions. This flexibility can promote greater consumer direction and choice.

Tapping housing wealth through reverse mortgages has the potential to fill some critical gaps in our nation's long-term care financing system. Most importantly, by liquidating home equity, seniors impaired by Alzheimer's can gain access to an important new source of funding to pay for services and supports at home.

To realize the potential of using home equity for long-term care, we will need to address many challenges. Currently, there is still little awareness of this product among seniors and Alzheimer's sufferers in general. Many older Americans are reluctant to take out a loan on their home after having spent many years paying off their mortgage.

Government incentives to reduce the up front cost of these loans may be able to play an important role in promoting such an approach to financing long-term care. The appropriate use of these funds—whether to purchase services or private insurance—also needs to be examined further to ensure that seniors make wise decisions with their limited housing resources. But with education and counseling, growing numbers of older Americans will be able to continue to live at home with dignity through the use of reverse mortgages.

If you are considering a reverse mortgage, it's important to get as much information as you can, and to consider all of your options.

For many older homeowners, selling your home and moving to a less expensive home is not always the best way to protect your assets for yourself and your family. However, a reverse mortgage can be just the opportunity that you've been looking for to take care of those substantial Alzheimer's care expenses.

●

I'M VERY PLEASED WITH EACH
ADVANCING YEAR. IT STEMS
BACK TO WHEN I WAS FORTY. I
WAS A BIT UPSET ABOUT
REACHING THAT MILESTONE,
BUT AN OLDER FRIEND
CONSOLED ME: "DON'T
COMPLAIN ABOUT GROWING
OLD — MANY, MANY PEOPLE
DO NOT HAVE THAT PRIVILEGE."
— EARL WARREN

4

LONG-TERM CARE OPTIONS

EACH YEAR, THOUSANDS OF FAMILIES IN THE United States face the difficult task of deciding when it's time to seek additional help in caring for a loved one with Alzheimer's disease. Perhaps your loved one can no longer care for himself or herself, has had a stroke or heart attack, or maybe your loved one has fallen and broken a hip, but no matter the reason, those involved are almost always under great stress. At times like these, it's important that you pause, take a deep breath and understand that there are things you can do. Good information is available and you can make the right choices for you and your loved one.

Americans are living longer than ever before. At the turn of the 20th century, the average life expectancy was about 47 years. As we enter the 21st century, life expectancy has almost doubled. As a result, we face more challenges and transitions in our lives than those who came before us. One of the most difficult transitions people face is the change from independent living in their own home or apartment to living in an assisted living facility or a nursing home. There are many reasons why this transition is so difficult. One is the loss of their home—a home where the person lived for many years with a lifetime of memories. Another is the loss of independence. Still another is the loss of the level of privacy we enjoy at home, since nursing home living is often shared with a roommate.

Early on, many people with Alzheimer's do well at home, especially when a spouse or other caregiver is present. As the disease progresses, however, some adult children have a parent with Alzheimer's move in with them. This can require modifying their house, schedule and life-style. Eventually, though, even the most loving and accommodating family may be unable to meet the needs of a person with Alzheimer's and they may need to think about long-term care options for their loved one.

Long-term care may mean help from family and friends or a regular visit by a home health aide. Or it may mean moving your loved one into an assisted living facility or a nursing home that can provide 24 hour medical attention. In fact, a variety of options are available, depending on where you live.

Selecting long-term care can be difficult, but determining your own needs and the needs of your loved one are the first steps in finding help.

SEEKING HELP

One obstacle you may need to overcome is your own reluctance to ask for help. You may be worried that your loved one won't feel comfortable with other caregivers. Maybe you think that no one else can provide care as well as you can. These reactions are common and, to some extent, may be valid. But getting assistance can make care-giving less burdensome, both physically and emotionally. This assistance can provide other resources and skills that you may not possess and can give you a chance to rejuvenate your care-giving. Your loved one may actually improve with the help of these other resources. This improvement can lower your stress level as a caregiver.

Once you come to terms with seeking help, a continuum of options may be available in your community.

These may include:

- RESPITE CARE. Respite services offer care for your loved one, giving you occasional time off from your duties. Community organizations or residential facilities frequently offer these services. The most common respite care programs are home health services and adult day services.

  - HOME HEALTH SERVICES. These services are provided in your home and vary from one organization to the next. The most common assistance involves personal care such as bathing, dressing and grooming and helping your loved one with eating and going to the bathroom. Some agencies also provide help with meal preparation and household chores. Most provide nursing care that may include injections of medications and assistance with wound care and medical equipment. Some agencies may also provide physical therapy.

Generally your relationship with an agency starts with a home visit by one of the agency's social workers or registered nurses to assess your needs. Arrangements for payment may be discussed at this time.

- ADULT DAY SERVICES. Also known as elder care programs, adult day services provide socialization and activities for adults in need of assistance. Some programs are specifically designed for people with Alzheimer's disease, and others are for all older adults.

  These programs are generally available during daytime hours, usually weekdays only, and offer a variety of services. Staff will lead various activities, such as music programs and support groups. Most will provide a lunchtime meal, and some will offer transportation to and from your home.

  Adult day services can be a wonderful opportunity for your loved one to spend time engaged in activities with other adults, such as cooking or baking, playing games, singing, watching movies and doing arts and crafts. You may wonder if your loved one would enjoy such an experience and would like being around a group of new people. The answer isn't always easy to gauge, but you may be pleasantly surprised at what your loved one finds enjoyable, even as the disease progresses.

- INFORMAL RESOURCES. Respite care may be available through informal resources as well. For example, family, friends or neighbors may be available to help. Also, some communities have in-home volunteers or professional caregivers to provide respite. These services may be contacted through the Alzheimer's Association, Area Agency on Aging, in-home health agencies or churches.

• RESIDENTIAL CARE OPTIONS. As your loved one experience the changes brought on by advancing Alzheimer's disease, he or she will require increasing amounts of assistance. At some point, you may decide to look into alternative housing options in your community.

You may find a wide range of residential care settings available in your community, but most fall into one of the following categories:

- RETIREMENT HOUSING. These settings — also known as senior apartments or senior living

— provide housing only. Residents usually have their own apartment or private room that includes a kitchen. Common areas are available for residents to socialize in, but generally, staff doesn't organize group activities. Also, staff members are usually not on-site 24 hours a day and may have little or no medical training. Retirement housing is not licensed.

This type of residential care setting may be appropriate for people in the early stages of Alzheimer's who can care for themselves independently and live alone safely but are unable to manage an entire house.

▪ ASSISTED LIVING. People who need help with personal care and require general guidance but don't need the specialized medical care of a nursing home may be well-suited for assisted-living facilities. These facilities — also known as board and care, group homes, community-based residential facilities or foster homes — are best for those who have moderate functional impairment, but who can still engage in such tasks as feeding themselves and getting in and out of chairs.

Assisted Living facilities are typically large complexes with apartments or townhouse-like units that feature shared or private bedrooms, shared dining and kitchen areas and communal living quarters. Staff members assist with personal care, provide housekeeping services and organize social activities and programs. Residents may participate in meal preparation, laundry and other tasks. Staff are sometimes trained in dementia care-giving techniques, but often don't have medical training. Nursing evaluations are usually available only on certain days of the week.

- NURSING HOME. If your loved one needs medical care, a nursing home may be the preferred option. These facilities provide room and board with 24 hour skilled care — care provided by a licensed nurse. A registered dietitian plans and monitors all meals, and staff members offer structured activity programs.

  Some nursing homes have special units for people with Alzheimer's disease. Sometimes these units are really just a part of the regular nursing home, but they occupy an area set aside for people with Alzheimer's. Other units have been designed so that the environment, activities, philosophy of care and staff training revolve around the special needs of people with Alzheimer's.

  This type of setting may be suitable for people in the middle to late stages of Alzheimer's. They may also be appropriate for people who are in the early stages of the disease, but who need skilled medical care.

- CONTINUING CARE RETIREMENT COMMUNITIES. These facilities, sometimes called life care centers, offer many services so that as the needs of your loved one change, he or she may receive more advanced levels of care within the same complex. These care communities provide a continuum of support from those who can live independently to those who need skilled nursing care. This type of facility offers your loved one the benefit of living in one place throughout the progression of his or her disease.

CHOOSING THE TYPE OF CARE

To decide which type of care would work best for you, assess the needs of your loved one and your needs as a caregiver. Ask your doctor, social worker, members of your local Alzheimer's Association chapter or another community agency to help you determine your loved one's potential needs. Any new care arrangement you make will involve blending your capabilities as a caregiver with the needs of your loved one.

Keep in mind that some settings aren't designed for people with Alzheimer's. And as the needs of your loved one change, care giving options may also change. Some settings may not be able to care for your loved one throughout the course of the disease. Most people require more support and help as the disease progresses.

To determine which type of care is best for your loved one, consider the following:

- Is 24-hour supervision needed?

- Does your loved one need special care? If so, what type of skills must a caregiver have to provide that care? For example, does your loved one have communication difficulties or unique behaviors, or does he or she need toileting and bathing assistance?

- Does your loved one want to walk or move around but needs direction and assistance?

- Does your loved one need help in taking medications?

- Does your loved one have complex medical problems, such as heart disease or diabetes?

- What kinds of programs and activities should the facility offer?

- What types of meals are needed? Do the meals need to be prepared by a caregiver?

- Do you want a facility that specializes in Alzheimer's care?

- How will the costs be covered?

The amount of care needed and type of atmosphere preferred will influence your decision as to which type of care setting you should visit.

EVALUATING A FACILITY

Once you have determined which arrangement would best meet the needs of your loved one, think about what questions you want to ask when you visit the facility. Set up an appointment with a staff person for your initial visit. This will ensure that someone will be available to answer your questions and give you a tour. Also, it's helpful to take along another family member or friend who also can ask questions and with whom you can share observations.

When you visit a facility, consider the following:

- Dedication to Alzheimer's care.
    - Is the facility committed to Alzheimer's care? If the facility is licensed, their most recent facility inspection report will highlight the type of care provided and will cite any areas that need improvement.

    - What is the facility's philosophy and mission? Ask for a description of the facility's philosophy and mission statement. This statement should address the special needs of people with Alzheimer's.

- What type of care is available throughout the stages of Alzheimer's?

- Does the facility serve only people with Alzheimer's?

• Specialized Care Plans
  - How are care plans created and how often are they updated? These assessments provide information on how to care for your loved one. They may include likes, dislikes, past interests, medical needs and preferred daily activities.

  - How are you informed of any care needs or changes?

  - How are daily needs monitored?

• Total care environment
  - Does the staff address the physical, emotional, spiritual and social needs of people with Alzheimer's?

  - How do staff members manage certain behaviors?

  - What is the policy on using physical restraints or medications to control behavior?

- How much individualized care and assistance is given?

- How is adequate nutrition provided? Ask for a copy of the weekly or monthly menu.

• Meaningful activities
  - Are meaningful group and individual activities offered throughout the day? Activities should be enjoyable, give your loved one a sense of usefulness and involve reminiscing about his or her past.

  - Do activities include tasks for daily living such as making the bed, brushing teeth and setting the table?

  - How are activities modified to meet the needs of people with Alzheimer's?

• Experienced Staff
  - What are the qualifications and experience of the staff?

  - Does the staff receive specialized Alzheimer's training?

  - How many staff members are present during the day, evening, night, weekend, and holiday hours?

- Home environment
  - Does the facility have a home-like feel to it?

  - Is the environment safe and well suited for people with Alzheimer's?

  - How does the facility ensure safety while also promoting independence?

  - Does the facility have an outdoor area for residents that is safe and secure?

Before you make a final decision, consider returning to the care setting without an appointment. It may also be beneficial to arrive at a different time of day from your first visit or on a weekend. See if your impressions are the same as when you toured with a staff member.

Keep in mind that most facilities have waiting lists, and it may be beneficial to explore your options early, before a crisis arises. This allows for a more thorough evaluation without additional pressure.

HOW TO PAY FOR ASSISTED LIVING OR NURSING HOME CARE

Most people who make the decision to move to assisted living or a nursing home do so during a time of great stress. Whatever the reason, the spouse or relative who helps a person transition during a time of stress faces the immediate dilemma of how to find the right facility. The task is no small one, and a huge sigh of relief can be heard when the right place is found and the loved one is moved into the assisted living facility or nursing home. For many, the most difficult task is just beginning: *How to cope with bills that may total $3,500 (assisted living) to $8,000 (nursing home)* per month to reside in the facility.

Paying for an assisted living facility or a nursing home is of major concern to most people. There are basically five ways that you can pay the cost of an assisted living facility or nursing home.

1. LONG TERM CARE INSURANCE

If you are fortunate enough to have this type of coverage, it may go a long way toward paying the cost of the nursing home. Unfortunately, long term care insurance has only started to become popular in the last few years and most people facing a nursing home stay do not have this coverage.

2. PAY WITH YOUR OWN FUNDS

This is the method many people are required to use at first. Quite simply, it means paying for the cost of a nursing home out of your own pocket. Unfortunately, with nursing home bills averaging between $6,000 and $8,000 per month in our area, few people can afford a long term stay in a nursing home.

3. VA Benefits

It is a well kept secret that Veteran's Benefits will pay for long term care in an assisted living or nursing home facility. This will be discussed in further detail in Chapter Five.

4. Medicare

This is the national health insurance program primarily for people 65 years of age and older, certain younger disabled people, and people with kidney failure. Medicare provides short term assistance with nursing home costs, but only if you meet the strict qualification rules.

5. Medicaid

This is a federal and state funded and state administered medical benefit program which can pay for the cost of the nursing home if certain asset and income tests are met. Our discussion will concentrate on Medicare and Medicaid in Chapter Six.

•

THE LONGER I LIVE THE MORE BEAUTIFUL LIFE BECOMES.
— Frank Lloyd Wright

5

VETERAN'S BENEFITS

THERE ARE A LARGE NUMBER OF SERVICES and benefits that have been made available to veterans and their family members who are deemed eligible for receiving them. This includes several medical services that are beneficial to veterans and their dependents and family members who suffer from Alzheimer's. This life-long benefit is considered a part of your earnings as a result of your service to the United States.

ELIGIBILITY

To begin with, all veterans are potentially eligible to receive benefits as long as they have had active service in the Army, Navy, Air Force, Marines, the Coast Guard, or (during World War II) the Merchant Marines, and have been discharged in conditions other than dishonorably. National Guard and Reservists who have been called to active duty by a Federal Executive Order may also be eligible for receiving veteran's benefits. Also, Reservists and National Guard members who are returning service members and have served active duty in several combat operations hold special eligibility for certain hospital care, medical services, and nursing home care within the two years that follow that active duty.

Veteran's Medical Benefits Package Overview

The following is the United States Military's description of the Medical Benefits Package offered to Veterans, with respect to Alzheimer's sufferers.

In October 1996, Congress passed the Veterans' Health Care Eligibility Reform Act of 1996. This legislation paved the way for the creation of a Medical Benefits Package - a standard enhanced health benefits plan generally available to all enrolled veterans. Like other standard health care plans, the Medical Benefits Package emphasizes preventive and primary care, offering a full range of outpatient and inpatient services.

The VA places a priority on improved veteran satisfaction and maintains that their goal is to ensure the quality of care and service that veterans receive is consistently excellent, in every location, in every program.

Here are some opportunities and requirements/limits for veterans' benefits:

Veterans Benefits

Opportunities:	Requirements/ Limits:
If you are a veteran, you might be able to get help paying for your long-term care needs.	You must be eligible for VA benefits and can only receive care in VA facilities.
The VA provides care in VA nursing homes and some at-home care.	There might be a waiting list for VA nursing homes

THE SOUL OF MAN IS IMMORTAL
AND IMPERISHABLE.
— PLATO

Services Covered Under The Medical Benefits Package

Basic Care

- Outpatient medical, surgical, and mental health care, including care for substance abuse.

- Inpatient hospital, medical, surgical, and mental health care, including care for substance abuse.

- Prescription drugs, including over-the-counter drugs and medical and surgical supplies available under the VA national formulary system.

- Emergency care in VA facilities.

Preventative Care

- Periodic medical exams.

- Health education, including nutrition education.

- Maintenance of drug-use profiles, drug monitoring, and drug use education.

- Mental health and substance abuse preventive services.

Services Not Covered Under The Medical Benefits Package

- Drugs, biologicals, and medical devices not approved by the Food and Drug Administration unless the treating medical facility is conducting formal clinical trials under an Investigational Device Exemption (IDE) or an Investigational New Drug (IND) application, or the drugs, biologicals, or medical devices are prescribed under a compassionate use exemption.

- Hospital and outpatient care for a veteran who is either a patient or inmate in an institution of another government agency if that agency has a duty to give the care or services.

SERVICES WITH LIMITED COVERAGE:

- A veteran may receive certain types of VA hospital and outpatient care not included in the Medical Benefits Package such as humanitarian emergency care for which the individual will be billed, compensation and pension examinations, dental care, readjustment counseling, care as part of a VA-approved research project, seeing-eye or guide dogs, sexual trauma counseling and treatment, special registry examinations.

- A veteran may receive VA hospital and outpatient care based on factors other than veteran status e.g., a veteran who is a private-hospital patient and is referred to VA for a diagnostic test by that hospital under a sharing contract; a veteran who is a VA employee and is examined to determine physical or mental fitness to perform official duties; Department of Defense retiree under a sharing agreement.

- A veteran may receive VA hospital and outpatient care outside the United States, without regard to the veteran's citizenship, if necessary for treatment of a service-connected disability, or any disability associated with and held to be aggravating a service-connected disability or if the care is furnished to a veteran participating in a VA rehabilitation program.

ASSISTED LIVING CARE

It is a well-kept secret that veteran's benefits are an excellent source of funds for long term care at an Assisted Living Facility or Nursing Home. This benefit is available to the veteran, spouse of the veteran, or the widow of a veteran. The divorced spouse is not eligible. The maximum monthly benefit for 2007 is from $1519 to $1801 for the veteran with one dependent and $976 for the widow(er). The qualifications for the program are as follows:

- Income does not exceed cost of the assisted living facility.

- Assets (not including house and life insurance) are less than $85,000.

- Applicant must be permanently and totally disabled and require care of assistance on a regular basis to protect the claimant from the hazards or dangers incident to his or her daily environment (a doctor's report may be required).

- Served during these time periods:

World War I

April 6, 1917, through November 11, 1918, extended to April 1, 1920, for those who served in Russia. Service after November 11, 1918 and before July 2, 1921, is considered World War I service if the veteran served in the active military, naval, or air service after April 5, 1917 and before November 12, 1918.

World War II

December 7, 1941, through December 31, 1946, extended to July 25, 1947, when continuous with active duty on or before December 31, 1946.

Korean War

June 27, 1950, through January 31, 1955.

Vietnam War

August 5, 1964, (February 28, 1961 for those who were in Vietnam) to May 7, 1975.

Persian Gulf War

August 2, 1990, to date yet to be determined.

Somalia, Bosnia, Kosovo

No dates have been set as of this writing.

•

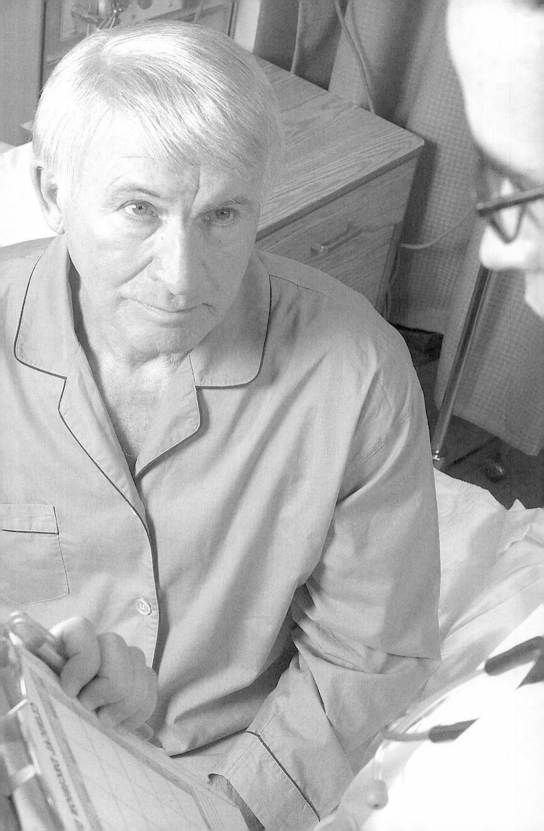

6

MEDICAID FOR PAYMENT OF AT HOME CARE, ASSISTED LIVING, AND NURSING HOME

THERE IS A GREAT DEAL OF CONFUSION about Medi*care* and Medi*caid*. Medicare is the federally funded and state administered health insurance program primarily designed for older individuals (i.e. those over age 65). There are some limited long-term care benefits that can be available under Medicare. In general, if you are enrolled in the traditional Medicare plan, and you've had a hospital stay of at least three days and are then admitted into a skilled nursing facility, Medicare may pay for a while. (If you are a Medicare Managed Care Plan beneficiary, a three day hospital stay may not be required to qualify.) If you qualify, traditional Medicare may pay the full cost of the nursing home stay for the first 20 days and can continue to pay the cost of the nursing home stay for the next 80 days, but with a daily deductible. Some Medicare supplement insurance policies will pay the cost of that deductible. For Medicare Managed Care Plan enrollees, there is no deductible for days 21 through 100, as long as the strict qualifying rules continue to be met.

So, in the best case scenario, the traditional Medicare or the Medicare Managed Care Plan may pay up to 100 days for each spell of illness. In order to qualify for this 100 days of coverage, however, the nursing home resident must be receiving daily skilled care and generally must continue to improve. (Note: Once the Medicare and Managed Care beneficiary has not received a Medicare covered level of care for 60 consecutive days, the beneficiary may again be eligible for the 100 days of skilled nursing coverage for the next spell of illness.)

WHAT IS MEDICAID?
Medicaid is a benefits program which is primarily funded by the federal government and administered by each state. Sometimes the rules can vary from state to state. One primary benefit of Medicaid is that, unlike Medicare (which only pays for skilled nursing), the Medicaid program will pay for long-term care in a nursing home once you've qualified.

Medicare does not pay for treatment for all diseases or conditions. For example, a long-term stay in a nursing home may be caused by Alzheimer's or Parkinson's disease, and even though the patient receives medical care, the treatment will not be paid for by Medicare. These stays are called custodial nursing stays and Medicare does not pay for custodial nursing home stays. In that instance, you'll either have to pay privately (i.e. use long-term care insurance or your own funds), or you'll have to qualify for Medicaid.

While it's never possible to predict at the outset how long Medicare will cover the rehabilitation, it usually falls far short of the 100 day maximum. Even if Medicare does cover the maximum period, what happens after that 100 days of coverage have been used?

At that point, the choices for coverage are: long-term care insurance, paying the bills with your own assets, or qualifying for Medicaid.

WHY SEEK ADVICE FOR MEDICAID?

As life expectancies rise, so do long-term care costs and the challenge becomes paying for them. Many people cannot afford $8,000 or more per month for the cost of a nursing home. Those who can may find their life savings wiped out in a matter of years, even months. This is where the Medicaid Program can help.

In our lifetime, Medicaid has become the long-term care insurance of the middle class. While eligibility to receive Medicaid benefits requires meeting certain guidelines concerning income and assets, ensuring that you don't put your family security in jeopardy requires planning and expert advice. For example, you need to ensure you have sufficient assets for the security of your loved ones in case they have a similar crisis. Without planning and advice, many people spend more than they should and their family security is jeopardized.

EXEMPT ASSETS AND COUNTABLE ASSETS: WHAT MUST BE SPENT?

Exempt assets are those which Medicaid will not take into account. These are the current, primary exempt assets:

- Home (equity up to $500,000). The home must be the principal place of residence of the spouse or there must be an intent to return home within six months by the nursing home resident.

- Personal belongings and household goods.

- One car for spouse.

- Burial spaces and irrevocable prepaid funeral contract.

- Value of life insurance if combined face value is $1,500 or less. If total face value exceeds $1,500, then the cash value of these policies is countable.

All other assets are generally *non-exempt*, and are countable. This includes:

- Cash, savings, and checking accounts, credit union share and draft accounts.

- Certificates of deposit.

- U.S. Savings Bonds.

- Individual Retirement Accounts (IRA), Keogh plans (401k, 403b).

- Nursing home accounts.

- Prepaid funeral contracts which can be canceled.

- Trusts (depending on the terms of the trust)

- Real estate (other than the residence).

- More than one car.

- Boats or recreational vehicles.

- Stocks, bonds, or mutual funds.

- Land contracts or mortgages held on real estate sold.

While the Medicaid rules themselves are complicated and tricky, it's safe to say that a single person will qualify for Medicaid as long as she has only exempt assets plus a small amount of cash and/or money in the bank (up to $1,500 in Ohio).

Some Common Questions

I've added my kids' names to our bank account. Do they still count?

Yes. The entire amount is counted unless you can prove some or all of the money was contributed by the other person who is on the account. This rule applies to cash assets such as:

- Savings and checking accounts

- Credit union share and draft accounts

- Certificates of deposit

- U.S. Savings Bonds

Can't I just give my assets away?

Many people wonder, can't I give my assets away? The answer is, maybe; but only if it's done just right. The law has severe penalties for people who simply give away their assets to create Medicaid eligibility. In Ohio, for example, every $5,247 (in 2007) given away during the three years prior to a Medicaid application creates a one month period of ineligibility. So even though the federal Gift Tax laws allow you to give away up to $12,000 per year *without gift tax consequences*, those gifts could result in a period of ineligibility for Ohio Medicaid of two months. Legislation enacted February 8, 2006, extends the look back period to five years (and in some ways the penalty period) and imposes new penalties for gifts made after February 8, 2006. Giving, under these new rules, may be possible; however, it is important to have the advice of an attorney well-versed in them.

Though some families do spend virtually all of their savings on nursing home care, Medicaid often does not require it. There are a number of strategies which can be used to protect family financial security.

ELDER CARE PLANNING FOR MARRIED COUPLES

Division of Assets is the name commonly used for the Spousal Impoverishment provisions of the Medicare Catastrophic Act of 1988. It applies only to couples. The intent of the law was to change the eligibility requirements for Medicaid when one spouse needs nursing home care while the other spouse remains in the community, i.e., at home. The law, in effect, recognizes that it makes little sense to impoverish both spouses when only one needs to qualify for Medicaid assistance for nursing home care. As a result of this recognition, division of assets was born. Basically, in a division of assets, the couple gathers all their countable assets together in a review. Exempt assets, discussed above, are not counted. The countable assets are then divided in two, with the at-home or community spouse allowed to keep one-half of all countable assets to a maximum of approximately $101,640. The other half of the countable assets must be spent down until less than $1,500 remains. The amount of the countable assets which the at-home spouse gets to keep is called the Community Spouse Resource Allowance (CSRA).

Each state also establishes a monthly income floor for the at-home spouse. This is called the Minimum Monthly Maintenance Needs Allowance. This permits the community spouse to keep a minimum monthly income ranging from about $1,711 to $2,541(in 2007). If the community spouse does not have at least $1,711 in income, then he or she is allowed to take the income of the nursing home spouse in an amount large enough to reach the Minimum Monthly Maintenance Needs Allowance (i.e., up to at least $1,711). The nursing home spouse's remaining income goes to the nursing home. This avoids the necessity (hopefully) for the at-home spouse to dip into savings each month, which would result in gradual impoverishment.

To illustrate, assume the at-home spouse receives $800 per month in Social Security. Also assume that her needs are calculated to be the minimum of $1,711. With her Social Security, she is $911 short each month.

$1,711 at-home spouse's monthly needs
        (determined by formula)
   800 at-home spouse's Social Security
$ 911 short fall

In this case, the community spouse will receive $911 (the shortfall amount) per month from the nursing home spouse's Social Security and the rest of the nursing home spouse's income will then go to pay for the cost of his care. This does not mean, however, that there are no planning alternatives which the couple can pursue. Consider the following case studies.

CASE STUDY ONE

**PLANNING FOR MARRIED COUPLES
(MEDICAID WITHOUT ANY SPEND-DOWN)**

Ralph and Alice were high school sweethearts who lived in Cleveland, Ohio, their entire adult lives. Two weeks ago, Ralph and Alice celebrated their 51st anniversary. Yesterday, Alice, who has Alzheimer's, wandered away from home. The police found her, hours later, sitting on a street curb, talking incoherently. They took her to a hospital. Now the family doctor has told Ralph that he needs to place Alice in a nursing home. Ralph and Alice grew up during the Depression. They always tried to save something each month. Their assets, totaling $100,000 (not including their house), are as follows:

Savings account $15,000
IRA (husband) 50,000
Money Market account 32,000
Checking account 3,000
Residence (no mortgage) 80,000

Ralph gets a Social Security check for $1500 each month; Alice's check is $450. His eyes fill with tears as he says, "At $6,000 to the nursing home every month, our entire life savings will be gone in less than three years!" What's more, he's afraid he won't be able to pay his wife's monthly bills, because a neighbor told him that the nursing home will be entitled to all of their Social Security checks.

There is good news for Ralph and Alice. It's possible he will get to keep his income and most of their assets and still have the state Medicaid program pay Alice's nursing home costs. The process may take a little while, but the end result will be worth it.

To apply for Medicaid, Ralph will have to go through the Department of Family and Job Services (DFJS). If he does things strictly according to the way DFJS tells him, he will only be able to keep about half of their assets (about $50,000) plus keep his income.

But the results can actually be much better than that. Ralph might be able to turn the spend-down amount of roughly $50,000 into an income stream for him that will increase his income and meet the Medicaid spend-down virtually right away. In other words, if handled properly, Alice may be eligible for Medicaid from the first month that she goes into the nursing home. Please note this will not work in every case. That's why it's important to have an Elder Law Attorney guide you through the system and the Medicaid process to find the strategies that will be most beneficial in your situation.

With the proper advice, Ralph may be able to keep most of what he and Alice have worked so hard for. This is possible because the law does not intend to impoverish one spouse because the other needs care in a nursing home. This is certainly an example where knowledge of the rules and how to apply them can be used to resolve Ralph and Alice's dilemma. Of course, proper elder care planning differs according to the relevant facts and circumstances of each situation as well as the state law.

CASE STUDY TWO

FINANCIAL GIFTS TO CHILDREN

After her 73 year old husband, Harold, suffers a paralyzing stroke, Mildred and her daughter, Joan, need advice. Dark circles have formed under Mildred's eyes. Her hair is disheveled. Joan holds her hand. "The doctor says Harold needs long-term care in a nursing home," Mildred says. "I have some money in savings, but not enough. I don't want to lose my house and all our hard-earned money. I don't know what to do." Joan has heard about Medicaid benefits for nursing homes, but doesn't want her mother left destitute in order for Harold to qualify for them. Joan wants to ensure that her father's medical needs are met, but she also wants to preserve Mildred's assets. "Can't Mom just give her money to me as a gift?" she asks. "Can't she give away $12,000 a year? I could keep the money for her so she doesn't lose it when Dad applies for Medicaid."

Joan has confused Federal Gift Tax law with the issue of asset transfers and Medicaid eligibility. A gift to a child in this case is actually a transfer, and Medicaid has very specific rules about transfers. At the time Harold applies for Medicaid, for gifts made prior to February 8, 2006, the state will look back three years to see if any gifts have been made. Gifts made after February 8, 2006 will be subject to a five year look-back. The state won't let you just give away your money or your property to qualify for Medicaid. Any gifts or transfers for less than fair market value that are uncovered in the look-back period will cause a delay in Harold's eligibility for Medicaid. In addition to the changes in the look-back period from three to five years, the new law also states that the penalty period on asset transfers will not begin until the Medicaid applicant is in the nursing home and already spent down. This will frustrate the gifting plans of most people. So what can Harold and Mildred do? They may be able to institute a gifting program, save a good portion of their estate, and still qualify for Medicaid. But they have to set it up just right. The new rules are very precise and demanding. You should consult a knowledgeable advisor on how this may be done. But remember, when it's given away, it's given away.

Studies have shown that windfall money received by gift, prize, or lawsuit settlement is often gone within three years. In other words, even when the children promise that money will be available when needed, their own emergencies may make them spend the money. You must consult a knowledgeable advisor on how to set a plan that complies with the law and achieves your goals.

WILL I LOSE MY HOME?

Many people who apply for medical assistance benefits to pay for nursing home care ask this question. For many, the home constitutes much or most of their life savings. Often, it's the only asset that a person has to pass on to his or her children.

Under the Medicaid regulations, the home is an unavailable asset and not taken into account when calculating Medicaid eligibility if:

• Equity is less than $500,000

- It is the principal place of residence for the spouse

- There is intent to return within six months by the nursing home resident.

In 1993, Congress passed a law that requires states to make attempts to recover the value of Medicaid payments made to nursing home residents. Estate recovery has dramatically changed in Ohio since the end of June 2005, and applies to more assets than just the probate estate. The State of Ohio can now pursue joint and survivorship, transfer on death, payable on death, life estates, and possibly beneficiaries under life insurance and annuities to recover payments made by Medicaid. Expert advice, both prior to applying for Medicaid and after approval, are more critical than ever to preserve assets for the beneficiaries of Medicaid recipients.

Medicaid rules constantly change. You should seek assistance from someone knowledgeable about the latest changes.

•

SURE I'M FOR HELPING THE ELDERLY. I'M GOING TO BE OLD MYSELF SOME DAY.
— LILLIAN CARTER
IN HER 80S

7

ESTATE PLANNING

PEACE OF MIND IS ONE OF THE BEST GIFTS you can give. Putting your estate in order to protect your loved ones before you die will save time, money and aggravation. Progressive illnesses such as Alzheimer's Disease also make it important to do your estate planning early.

Alzheimer's Disease is an illness of dementia. As it progresses, it causes sufferers to lose their memories, their ability to reason, and their ability to understand the consequences of their decisions. Most people in the early stages of Alzheimer's disease can still execute advance directives or other estate planning documents. As the disease progresses, however, they become less able to manage their own affairs.

Once an individual with Alzheimer's has lost competence, it is too late to designate the person he or she wants to make his or her health care, financial, and estate planning decisions.

Choosing this decision maker in advance of incapacity is critical to maintaining continuity in decision making, thus maintaining the most favorable quality of life possible throughout the course of the disease.

For individuals with Alzheimer's Disease, empowering family members or trusted friends to make health care decisions (health care proxy) and to do estate and financial planning (power of attorney) ensures that the care-giving effort won't freeze up due to a lack of resources or the absence of a decision maker.

The proper execution of advance directives and a financial power of attorney is often a critical component of any Alzheimer's care plan.

In the next few chapters, we will discuss some exceedingly powerful estate planning tools such as:

- Last Will and Testament

- Trusts

- Durable Financial Power of Attorney

- Health Care Power of Attorney

- Living Will and Do Not Resuscitate Order

•

GOD GIVES EVERY BIRD ITS
FOOD, BUT HE DOES NOT
THROW IT INTO ITS NEST.
—J. G. HOLLAND

8

LAST WILL AND TESTAMENT

ONE OF THE BASICS OF ESTATE PLANNING is the use of a Last Will and Testament. The will is a legal document that will address important issues such as your beneficiaries, the distribution of your assets, and your executor (or executrix). A will can also appoint a guardian for you if you become incapacitated or a guardian for your disabled (or young) children.

The will can prevent the possibility of your estate being drained by legal bills. It absolutely must spell out how and to whom you want your property distributed as specifically as possible. The will must be signed by you in front of two witnesses.

A will can be made by any one who has property, is 18 years old, and is of sound mind and memory. It is crucial that anyone suffering from Alzheimer's contact his legal counsel as soon as diagnosis is made to properly prepare a Will before he is unable to do so.

The will can be changed at any time, as long as you are of sound mind and memory, by simply adding a codicil to the original will.

If you should die without a will (intestate), the probate court will appoint an administrator to distribute your assets according to the law. The probate court cannot follow your wishes if they don't know what they are.

If you've been told that you have dementia or Alzheimer's disease, you need to see an attorney before you write your will. The attorney may ask your doctor about your dementia. The attorney needs to make sure you can understand what the Will means. The attorney can also help you write your will.

There are several things you need to think about before you visit the attorney. You may want to ask a friend or a member of your family for help.

Work out how much money you have and how much your house, pension, car, etc. is worth. Subtract any money you owe — this may include loans, your mortgage, credit cards, etc.

Think about to whom you want to give your money and belongings when you die. You may want to include friends and family. You can also decide to give money to a charity.

Think about who you want to carry out your will when you die (this person is called an executor). You may want to take a friend with you when you see your attorney.

Once the will is written, read through it carefully before you sign and date it. Keep your will safe. If, at any time, you wish to change your will, ask your attorney for assistance.

●

CALL ON GOD, BUT ROW AWAY
FROM THE ROCKS.
— INDIAN PROVERB

9

TRUST PLANNING

THERE ARE NUMEROUS TRUSTS THAT ARE available for estate planning and to protect your assets — but too many to detail here. We will limit our discussion to:

- Living Trust

- Testamentary Trust

- Irrevocable trust

- Special Needs Trust

LIVING TRUST
The Living Trust is a revocable living trust. It is sometimes referred to as a revocable inter vivos trust, or a grantor trust. A living trust may be amended or revoked by the person creating it (commonly known as a trustor,

grantor, or settlor) at any time during the trustor's lifetime, as long as the trustor is competent.

A trust is a written legal agreement between the individual creating the trust and the person or institution named to manage the assets held in the trust (the "trustee"). In many cases, it is appropriate for you to be the initial trustee of your living trust, until management assistance is anticipated or required.

IN A LIVING TRUST AGREEMENT

- The trustee is given the legal right to manage and control the assets held in the trust.

- The trust provides for the persons or charitable organizations ("beneficiaries") who are to receive the income and principal on or after the trustor's death.

- The trustee is given guidance and certain powers and authority to manage and distribute the trust property in a prudent fashion.

- The trustee is a *fiduciary*. A fiduciary is one who occupies a position of trust and confidence and is subject to strict responsibilities, usually higher standards of performance than one who is dealing with his or her own property. Without the trustor's express written permission, the trustee cannot use trust property for the trustee's own personal use, benefit or self-interest. One must hold the trust property solely for the benefit of the beneficiaries of the trust.

A living trust can be an important part — in many cases, *the most important part*— of your estate plan. A living trust can provide for the private management of your assets if you choose not to act as trustee, or when you are unable to do so, by the person or persons whom you appoint as trustee. When you are incapacitated, your trustee can assume responsibility for your assets in an accountable fashion, and manage them for your benefit without direct court intervention or supervision. At your death, the trustee acts much as an executor would, gathering your assets, paying valid debts and claims and taxes, and distributing your assets as you have directed in your living trust.

Not everyone should have a living trust; however, the greater the risk of incapacity or death, the greater the need. Therefore, in the case of Alzheimer's sufferers, a Living Trust is a wise choice.

If you are acting as trustee of your own living trust and become incapacitated, whomever you have named as your successor trustee will assume the responsibility for managing your assets on your behalf. If your assets are not in your living trust, someone else must manage them. How this is accomplished may depend on whether the assets are your separate or community property.

Assets held in your living trust at your death can be managed by the trustee of your living trust and distributed in accordance with your directions in the trust. The trustee is also accountable to your beneficiaries for the trust assets held for their benefit after your death.

The trust is not under the direct management of the probate court either before or after your death and, therefore, the value and the nature of your assets and the identity of your beneficiaries do not become public record. At your death, however, notice must be given to all of your heirs and to all beneficiaries of your living trust, advising them, among other things, of their right to obtain a copy of the living trust.

If your assets were in your name alone at your death, then they would be subject to probate. At your death, a petition is filed with the court, usually by the person or institution named in your Will as executor. After notice is given and a hearing is held, your will is admitted to probate and an executor is appointed. A full inventory of the assets held in your name alone at your death is filed with the court and the probate continues until your estate is ready for distribution and the court approves the final distribution of your estate. Probate can take more time to complete than the distribution of your trust following your death. Assets held in a living trust can be more readily accessible to beneficiaries than those in a probate case. The cost of probate is often greater than the cost incurred by a comparable estate managed and distributed under a living trust. Probate is also time consuming and public record.

As noted, many people act as their own trustee until their incapacity or death. Others determine that they need financial assistance and management of their assets simply because they are too busy or too inexperienced or simply don't wish to have the responsibility of day-to-day management of their financial affairs.

Perhaps the most important decision for you to consider is your choice of a trustee to act in your place. As you have read, your trustee will have considerable authority and responsibility, is not under direct court supervision, and will assume that responsibility either during your lifetime (if you so choose), if you become incapacitated, or at your death.

A trustee may be a spouse, adult children, other relatives, family friends, business associates or a professional fiduciary. The professional fiduciary may be a bank or trust company which must be licensed by the state. You may also provide for co-trustees. There are a number of issues to consider. For example, will the appointment of one of your adult children cause undue stress in his or her relationship with siblings? What conflicts of interest are created if a business associate or partner is named as your trustee? Will the person named as successor trustee have the time, organizational ability and experience to do the job effectively?

Because living trusts are not under direct court supervision, a trustee who does not act in your best interests or in a prudent fashion accountable to you or your beneficiaries may be able to take advantage of the situation in some cases. A trustee under direct court supervision may be safeguarded by such things as court accountings or a bond.

Once created, the trust must be funded. The funding of a trust is simply the transfer of assets from your own name to whomever is acting as trustee of your living trust - be that you or some other person. Deeds to real property must, therefore, be prepared and recorded, bank accounts transferred, and stock and bond accounts or certificates transferred as well. These are not necessarily expensive tasks, but they are important ones and require some paperwork to complete in order to make your trust effective.

People in certain businesses (like real estate development) sometimes find that having a living trust creates excessive problems in the operation of the business when it is necessary to deal with a third party such as a title company.

If you have a living trust, you still need a will. Your will affects any assets which, for one reason or another, were held in your name alone at your death and were not in either your living trust or some other form of ownership. With the living trust, your will usually contains as its primary provision for the distribution of your estate, a *pour over* provision, which directs that any assets held in your name be transferred at your death to your living trust. Probate is not avoided with respect to those assets which are transferred to your living trust by your will.

A living trust will not pay income taxes during your lifetime. For so long as you are either the trustee or a co-trustee, no income tax returns are required to be filed for your living trust. The taxpayer identification number for the trust is your Social Security number, and all income and deductions related to the assets held in the trust are reportable on your individual income tax returns. When you are no longer a co-trustee of your trust, then information returns must be filed, reporting all of the income and deductions relating to the trust assets to the IRS and attributing them to your personal return; no additional tax is assessed by reason of the living trust. After your death, the income taxation of the living trust is similar to that applicable to a probate estate.

TESTAMENTARY TRUST

Another type of trust is the Testamentary Trust. Testamentary trusts are trusts which are created in your will and which, therefore, cannot provide for any management of your assets during your lifetime. Testamentary trusts can, however, provide for young children, disabled children, and others who need management of their assets after your death. The problem with the Testamentary Trust is that the person must die, his estate has to be probated, and then the Testamentary Trust is created. Attorneys in the past used these trusts extensively, but most experienced estate planning attorneys have now found that Special Needs Trusts and the Living Trust are more functional and beneficial.

IRREVOCABLE TRUST

Irrevocable trusts are trusts which, immediately upon their creation, are not amendable or revocable by you. These are generally tax-sensitive documents. Some examples include irrevocable life insurance trusts, irrevocable trusts for children and charitable trusts.

Once your trust has been signed, a very important task remains to be accomplished. In order to achieve your objectives of avoidance of court-supervised conservatorship proceedings if you are incapacitated or probate at your death, assets must be transferred to the trustee of the living trust. This is known as funding the trust.

A living trust can hold both separate and community property. If community property is held in a living trust, then both spouses are the grantors. Care must be taken to carefully designate the property held in a living trust by married persons as either separate or community property. Usually two trusts are used to keep the property separate and, if it is community property, then each spouse will put one-half interest into each of their trusts.

If you own real estate in another state, it is appropriate to transfer title for that asset to your trust, to avoid probate in the other state; you should consult with a lawyer in that state to prepare the deed and to advise you with respect to such a transfer. You may also contact your attorney here and he should be able to recommend a reputable attorney in another state with whom he has worked previously. Your attorney may be able to handle this transfer directly with that attorney for you.

Your lawyer can also advise you as to the title and process of transferring other assets. For example, you should consider changing beneficiary designations on life insurance to the trust. Changing beneficiary designations on a qualified retirement plan, such as a 401(k) or IRA, can create serious income tax issues and require the advice of a qualified professional.

You should consult with a qualified estate planning lawyer to assist you in the preparation of a living trust, a will, and other estate planning documents. While other professionals and business representatives may be involved in your estate planning process, legal documents should only be prepared by a qualified lawyer.

SPECIAL NEEDS TRUST

A special needs trust, also known as a supplemental needs trust, is created and established for the benefit of the disabled child or individual whose disability will continue for an indefinite period of time.

The trust is used to protect the assets a disabled individual would inherit from his parents or family. The trust may be funded by an insurance policy. This trust was not intended to supersede or replace government benefits such as Medicaid or SSI; it supplements the benefits the disabled individual is eligible for rather than reducing them. Principal and income from the trust is not considered a resource under any assistance or government program.

The trust gives complete control to the trustee to make distributions of the income and principal for the sole benefit of the disabled child. The distributions do not go directly to the individual, but can pay for such items as vacations, social events, and even medical care if the government benefit does not allow certain medical treatment. The trust can pay for a home and rent it to the individual. It can pay for repairs, utilities, and taxes; or buy furniture and a TV. It can pay funeral costs. The trust can also pay for legal services if these are not provided by another government agency. The basic rule is that money from the trust cannot be used for basic needs under Medicaid and SSI rules. Government benefits would be reduced if the disabled person were to receive money for housing, food or clothing.

There is another special needs trust that is used when a disabled individual has been awarded a medical malpractice suit or a personal injury settlement. Only the disabled person's parent, grandparent, legal guardian, or court is sanctioned to set up this type of trust. Provisions are typically made in the trust for successor trustees and the distribution of the remainder of the principal and income.

Making the trust irrevocable protects the principal and income from both your creditors and the disabled individual's creditors. If this trust is set up properly it will be completely separate from your estate. It will have its own tax identification number.

Should an individual with Alzheimer's suddenly find himself unable to manage the special needs trust, this type of trust will continue to function without interruption for the benefit of the disabled individual. Advance planning is vital.

•

PRAY AS IF EVERYTHING
DEPENDED UPON GOD AND
WORK AS IF EVERYTHING
DEPENDED UPON MAN.
— FRANCIS CARDINAL
    SPELLMAN

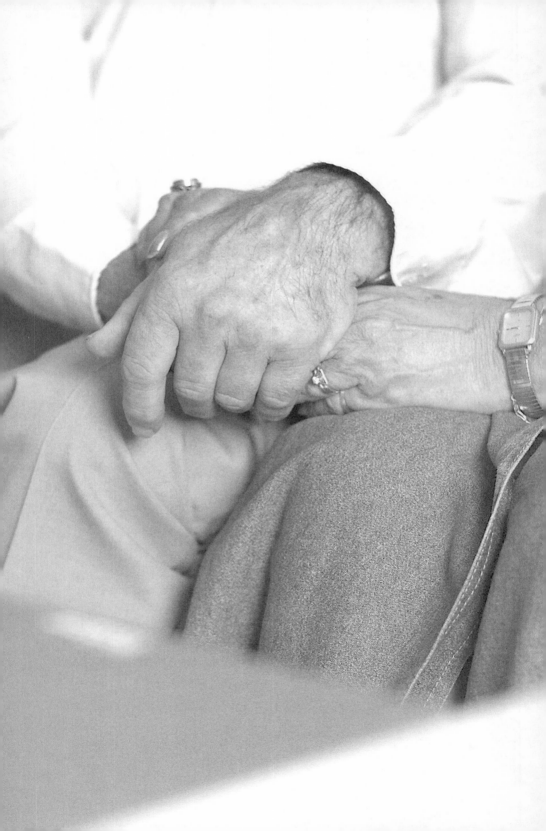

10

FINANCIAL DURABLE POWERS OF ATTORNEY

IN THE CASE OF MENTAL INCAPACITATION, such as with Alzheimer's disease, you'll need what is known as durable powers of attorney for finances and medical care. Ordinary powers of attorney automatically end if the person who makes them loses mental capacity; thus, they are *non*-durable. Durable power of attorney simply means that the document stays in effect if you become incapacitated and unable to handle matters on your own.

DURABLE POWER OF ATTORNEY FOR FINANCES
Some financial powers of attorney are very simple and used for single transactions, such as closing real estate deals. But the power of attorney we're discussing here is comprehensive; it's designed to let someone else manage all of your financial affairs for you if you become incapacitated. It's called a *durable power of attorney for finances* and is a critical tool in any estate plan.

With a durable power of attorney for finances, you can give a trusted person you name as much authority over your finances as you like. This person is usually called your agent or attorney-in-fact, though he or she most definitely does not have to be an attorney.

Your agent can handle mundane tasks such as sorting through your mail and depositing your Social Security checks, as well as more complex jobs like watching over your retirement accounts and other investments, or filing your tax returns. Your agent doesn't have to be a financial expert; just someone you trust completely who has a good dose of common sense. If necessary, your agent can hire professionals (paying them out of your assets) to help out.

The durable power of attorney for finances must willingly be signed and dated by the individual, then be notarized and witnessed by two people unrelated to the individual who must also sign and date the document.

Not all durable financial power of attorneys are equal. Your durable financial power of attorney should have gifting provisions and special language that would allow your attorney-in-fact to make gifts of your money and assets to your designated children, friends, your trust or any one else that you would designate. This is extremely important when you are doing estate planning.

A durable power of attorney for finances doesn't require a lawyer. Although you may purchase a power of attorney at a local stationery store, there are several types available such as springing powers of attorney and powers with gifting provisions. These documents must be specific to your state and must contain certain language that will let your agent handle your financial situation in the manner that you intend. It is crucial that an attorney be consulted to ensure that you get the correct document to suit your needs. The impact of having a durable power of attorney for finances is large. *Not* having one can be devastating to your estate planning.

If you don't create durable powers of attorney and something happens to you, your loved ones may have to go to court to get the authority to handle your affairs. Durable powers of attorney avoid guardianship and conservatorship.

GUARDIANSHIP

A guardianship is established through probate court by appointing an individual to make personal decisions for someone who is not able to make decisions for himself. A family member or friend initiates the proceeding by filing a petition in the circuit court in the county where the individual resides. A medical examination by a licensed physician is necessary to establish the mental capacity of the individual. A judge then declares that the person does not have the necessary mental capacity to care for his or her personal needs and appoints a guardian to make personal decisions for the individual. Unless limited by the court, the guardian has the same rights, powers and duties over the individual as parents have over their minor children. The guardian is required to report to the court on an annual basis.

CONSERVATORSHIP

A conservatorship is a legal relationship in which the probate court gives a person (the conservator) the power to make financial decisions for another (the protectee). The court proceedings are similar to those of a guardianship except that no medical examination is required before the judge determines if the individual has the capacity to manage his or her financial affairs and appoints a conservator to make financial decisions. Often the court appoints the same person to act as both guardian and conservator. Like the guardian, the conservator is required to report to the court on an annual basis.

Having durable powers of attorney for finance in place is preferable to having to file for guardianship and conservatorship. If, however, you become incapacitated and do not already have a durable power of attorney for finances, your family may have no choice but to begin guardianship and conservatorship proceedings.

By signing a durable power of attorney for finances now, you can determine who will be able to make financial decisions for you in the future should you be unable to make them for yourself.

The durable power of attorney for finances is an excellent tool to avoid court involvement and the cost and hardship of court proceedings. Since, probate court is open to the public, the durable powers of attorney for finances will also keep your life (and any problems you might face) private.

•

THE GREAT SECRET THAT ALL
OLD PEOPLE SHARE IS THAT
YOU REALLY HAVEN'T CHANGED
IN 70 OR 80 YEARS. YOUR BODY
CHANGES, BUT YOU DON'T
CHANGE AT ALL.
— DORIS LESSING

11

HEALTH CARE POWER OF ATTORNEY & LIVING WILL

A POWER OF ATTORNEY FOR HEALTH CARE and a living will are commonly referred to as advance directives.

A power of attorney for health care can eliminate much pain on the part of your loved ones. If you should become terminally ill or injured in an accident, and you don't wish to be kept alive by artificial means, a power of attorney for health care enables you to authorize named individuals to make medical decisions on your behalf.

A power of attorney for healthcare states whom you have chosen to make health care decisions for you. It becomes active any time you are unconscious or unable to make medical decisions.

If you are left unable to tell your doctors what kind of medical treatment you want, you need to have an alternate plan established. No one likes to consider such grim possibilities, but the truth is that almost every Alzheimer's family will eventually face this kind of difficulty. While medical powers of attorney can't prevent accidents or keep you young, they can certainly make life easier for you and your family if times get tough.

A living will informs your doctors that you should not be kept alive by artificial means for any extended period of time if you have a terminal condition or were in a permanent unconscious state. If you mark a specific box in the living will, all nutrition and hydration may be withheld. This document also makes it clear that any physician making a decision to terminate life support would notify the persons you have named therein. It also instructs the hospital not to put you on life support if there isn't reasonable expectation of recovery.

Your health care agent will work with doctors and other health care providers to make sure you get the kind of medical care you wish to receive. Health care agents may also be called your *health care proxy, health care surrogate,* or something similar, depending on where you live. When arranging your care, your agent is legally bound to follow your treatment preferences to the extent that he or she knows about them.

Without a power of attorney for healthcare and living will, you will remain on life support for a minimum of a year before the court will make the decision to take you off life support.

A power of attorney for healthcare and living will should be signed by the individual and two witnesses who: are unrelated to the individual, are not the agent, will not inherit from the individual, and are not involved in providing health care for the individual.

DNR Order

The power of attorney for healthcare also provides for a do not resuscitate (DNR) order, another kind of advance directive. A DNR is a request not to have cardiopulmonary resuscitation (CPR) if your heart stops or if you stop breathing. Unless given other instructions, hospital staff will try to help all patients whose heart has stopped or who have stopped breathing. You can use an advance directive form or tell your doctor that you don't want to be resuscitated. In this case, a DNR order is put in your medical chart by your doctor. DNR orders are accepted by doctors and hospitals in all states but because of specific laws in each state, you must use a form that is specific to your state.

A DNR order does not mean *do not treat*. Rather, it means that physicians, nurses and others will not initiate such emergency procedures as CPR, mouth-to-mouth resuscitation, external chest compression, electric shock, insertion of a tube to open the patient's airway, injection of medication into the heart, or provide open chest heart massage. Other treatments (such as antibiotic therapy, treatment for discomfort or pain, transfusions, dialysis, or use of a ventilator) may still be provided if needed.

If the patient is in a nursing home, a DNR order instructs the staff to neither perform emergency resuscitations nor to transfer the patient to a hospital for such procedures. It is widely recognized by health care professionals, clergy, lawyers and others that DNR orders are medically and ethically appropriate under certain circumstances. For some patients, CPR offers more burdens than benefits, and may be contrary to their wishes.

The success of CPR depends on the patient's overall medical condition and level of functioning before hospitalization. Age alone is not a predictor of success, although illnesses and frailties associated with advanced age often result in less successful outcomes. When successful, Cardiopulmonary resuscitation (CPR) restores heartbeat and breathing, enabling a patient to resume his or her previous life-style. When unsuccessful, CPR fails totally to restore basic life functions. When partially successful, CPR may restore heartbeat and breathing but leave the patient brain-damaged or otherwise impaired.

All adult patients are legally allowed to request a DNR order. If a person is already in a progressed stage of Alzheimer's and incapable of deciding about resuscitation, a family member or others close can decide on their behalf. Your physician must obtain your consent before entering a DNR order in your record if you are mentally capable of deciding, unless a discussion about CPR and your condition would cause you severe harm. In an emergency, it is assumed that all patients would consent to CPR unless a DNR order is in the record.

An adult patient in a hospital or nursing home can consent to a DNR order orally as long as two witnesses are present. One witness must be a physician. You can also make your wishes known before or during hospitalization in writing, before any two adults who must sign your statement as witnesses. A living will may also be used to convey these wishes as long as it is properly executed and witnessed.

You can specify that you want a DNR order only under certain circumstances (such as if you become terminally ill or permanently unconscious) or that you wish only specific CPR procedures performed such as mouth-to-mouth breathing, but not open heart massage.

Before making a decision about CPR, you should speak with your physician about your overall health and the benefits and burdens CPR would provide for you. A full and early discussion between you and your doctor can avoid later misunderstandings.

If you don't want to be resuscitated and you request a DNR order, your physician must either:

- Enter the order in your chart; or

- Transfer responsibility for your care to another physician; or

- Refer the matter to a dispute mediation system in the hospital or nursing home. The mediation system is only authorized to mediate disputes; it cannot overrule your decision.

If mediation has not resolved the dispute within 72 hours, your physician must enter the order or transfer you to the care of another physician.

You are presumed by law to be mentally capable of deciding about CPR unless two physicians or a court determine that you no longer have the capacity to make the decision. In the case of an Alzheimer's patient, you will likely be monitored relatively regularly by a doctor, and your ability to make the decision will be known. You will be informed of this determination if you are able to understand it, and no DNR order will be written if you object.

If you lose the capacity to decide and did not leave advance instructions, a DNR order can be entered only with the consent of someone chosen by you in advance, or by a family member or someone with a close personal relationship to you. The person highest on the following list will decide on your behalf:

- A person you have selected to decide about resuscitation

- A court-appointed guardian (if there is one)

- Your closest relative

- A close friend.

If you are a patient in a hospital or nursing home, you can appoint a person orally, with two witnesses present.

You can also appoint someone during or in advance of hospitalization by stating your wishes in writing and signing and dating that statement with any two adults present. The adults must also sign your written statement.

A family member or close friend can consent to a DNR order only when you are unable to decide for yourself and:

- You have a terminal condition

- You are permanently unconscious

- CPR would be medically futile

- CPR would impose an extraordinary burden on you given your medical condition and the expected outcome of resuscitation

- Anyone deciding for you must base the decision on your wishes, including your religious and moral beliefs, or if your wishes are not known, in your best interest

If your family disagrees, they can ask for the matter to be mediated. Your physician will request mediation if he or she is aware of such disagreement among family members.

If you lose the capacity to decide and have not selected anyone to decide on your behalf, a DNR order can be entered only if two physicians conclude that CPR would be medically useless or if a court approves the DNR order. It would be best if you discuss the matter with your physician and leave instructions in advance.

If you change your mind after consenting to the DNR order, you or anyone who consents to a DNR order on your behalf, can withdraw that consent at any time by informing your physician, nurses, or others of the decision.

If you have a DNR order and are transferred between a nursing home and a hospital, the health facility to which you are sent may continue the DNR order, but is not obligated to do so. If the order is not continued, you or your selected decision maker will be informed and can request that the order be entered again.

•

12

AVOIDING PROBATE

PROBATE COURT WILL APPOINT A GUARDIAN or conservator for you if you are unable to make medical or financial decisions. Probate court will also probate your last will and testament at your death. Probating an estate is time consuming, costly and, of course, all records are public. Your neighbors and friends can access your estate records. There is no privacy.

The trust is only one tool that will help you avoid probate. Transfer on death or payable on death designations are two more estate planning tools that avoid probate. You can designate the beneficiary on a life insurance policy, IRAs, retirement plans, annuities, checking and savings accounts, deeds for your property and titles for your vehicles. Assets that are designated transfer on death or payable on death will not be distributed according to your Last Will and Testament and will, therefore, avoid probate.

Seek advice from a qualified legal advisor regarding tax implications and suitable estate planning options.

•

13

PROFESSIONAL
SERVICES

A PERSON WITH ALZHEIMER'S AND THEIR family members face many unique legal issues. As you can tell from our discussion of the Medicaid program, the legal, financial, and care planning issues facing the prospective nursing home resident and family can be particularly complex. If you or a family member need nursing home care, it is clear that you need expert legal help. Where can you turn for that help?

It is difficult for the consumer to be able to identify lawyers who have the training and experience required to provide expert guidance during this most difficult time. Generally, nursing home planning and elder care planning is an aspect of the services provided by elder law attorneys. Consumers must be cautious in choosing a lawyer.

Before retaining any professional to assist you with your estate and financial planning, you should inquire about that individual's qualifications. In addition, you should determine whether the professional advisor has any underlying financial incentive to sell you a particular investment, such as an annuity or life insurance policy, because that financial incentive may color the advice given to you. A living trust is often held out as an enticement or loss leader by offices which are not staffed with competent and qualified estate planning lawyers. Unfortunately, some sellers of dubious financial products gain the confidence and private financial information of their victims by posing as providers of trust or estate planning services.

Some lawyers who work in the estate planning area are *certified specialists in estate planning, trust and probate law.* This designation means that they have met standards for certification set by that state's bar association. However, not all lawyers who have experience and expertise in estate planning have sought that certification.

If you do not already know a lawyer who is qualified to help with your living trust, obtain referrals from someone whose judgment you can trust — friends, associates or your employer. Your local bar association maintains a list of State Bar certified lawyer referral services in your area. You should be wary of organizations or offices who are staffed by non-lawyer personnel and who promote *one size fits all* living trusts or living trust kits. A living trust created by someone who is not a qualified lawyer can have enormous and costly consequences for your estate and may not achieve your goals and objectives. Do not allow yourself to be pressured into immediately purchasing a living trust or any other estate planning product.

Hospital social workers, and other support groups, accountants, and other financial professionals can also be good sources of recommendations.

To have the issues addressed properly, you need a lawyer who devotes a substantial part of his or her practice to nursing home planning. Don't hesitate to ask the lawyer what percentage of his practice involves nursing home planning. You may also choose to ask how many new nursing home planning cases the law office handles each month. There is no correct answer. But there is a good chance that a law office that assists with two nursing home placements a week is likely to be more up-to-date and knowledgeable than an office that helps with two placements a year.

Ask whether the lawyer is a member of any elder law planning organizations. Is the lawyer involved with committees or local or state bar organizations that have to do with nursing home planning? Does the lawyer lecture on nursing home planning? If so, to whom? (For example, if the lawyer is asked to teach other lawyers about elder law and nursing home planning, that is a very good sign that the lawyer is considered to be knowledgeable by people who should know.) If the lawyer lectures to the public, you might try to attend one of the seminars. This should help you decide if this is the lawyer for you.

When you retain a lawyer, you should understand what services are to be provided and how much they will cost. You should indicate your understanding of the terms and conditions of the lawyer's employment with a fee agreement prepared by your lawyer.

Remember, there are many who call themselves *trust specialists, certified planners* or other titles which are intended to suggest that the person has received advanced training in estate planning. America is experiencing an explosion of promotions by unqualified individuals and entities which have only one real goal — to gain access to your finances in order to sell insurance-based products such as annuities and other commission-based products.

Here are some helpful hints and suggestions:

- Before considering a living trust or any other estate or financial planning document or service, consult with a lawyer or other financial advisor who is knowledgeable in estate planning, and who is not trying to sell a product which may be unnecessary.

- Always ask for time to consider and reflect on your decision. Do not allow yourself to be pressured into purchasing any estate or financial planning product.

- Know your cancellation rights.

- Be wary of home solicitors who insist on receiving confidential and detailed information about your assets and finances.

- Find out if any complaints have been filed against the company by calling local and state consumer protection offices or the Better Business Bureau.

- Know to whom you are talking, insist on identification, and ask for a description of his or her qualifications, education, training and expertise in the field of estate planning.

- Always ask for a copy of any document you sign at the time it is signed.

- Report high-pressure tactics, misrepresentations or fraud to the police immediately.

When you retain a lawyer, you should understand what services are to be provided and how much they will cost.

In the end, follow your instincts and choose an attorney who knows this area of the law, who is committed to helping others, and who will listen to you and the unique wants and needs of you and your family.

•

BEWARE OF THE YOUNG DOCTOR
AND THE OLD BARBER.
— BENJAMIN FRANKLIN

14

CONCLUSION

IT'S NORMAL TO OCCASIONALLY FORGET a phone number, the day of the week, or what you just came in to a room to do. Memory changes, confusion, and disorientation associated with Alzheimer's Disease, however, grow progressively worse over time. Early-stage warning signs may develop gradually and go unnoticed, or, in many cases, initially be mistaken for the normal aging process.

When behavioral situations point strongly toward, or suggest Alzheimer's, it's wise to seek diagnosis quickly, and then begin preparations as early into the progression of the disease as can be managed.

According to the Centers for Disease Control and Prevention, Alzheimer's is the 11th leading cause of death for adults age 65 and older. While the cause of Alzheimer's disease is still uncertain, researchers agree that the risk of developing the condition increases as a person ages.

It's estimated that 4 million Americans have Alzheimer's Disease and, unless a cure or significant treatment is found, it's predicted that as many as 14 million will have the disease by 2050. To better help ourselves and/or our loved ones, all of us can benefit from knowing what the most common early-stage warning signs of Alzheimer's are.

If you or someone you love experiences any of the symptoms listed below, see your physician. A medical examination is the first and most important step if you suspect you or someone close to you might have Alzheimer's.

- Recent memory loss that impairs the person's ability to complete routine assignments at work and/or function effectively at home: May frequently forget names, phone numbers and work tasks and have trouble remembering them even when reminded.

- Problems with language: May progressively forget simple words, substitute inappropriate words, and/or make statements that don't make sense.

- Disorientation in time and space and getting confused or lost in a familiar place: May leave their home and then forget where they intended to go, could become lost on a nearby street and not know how to get home.

- Difficulty completing familiar tasks: May, for example, prepare a meal but forget to serve it— or even forget that they ever made it.

- Distorted judgment: May dress inappropriately, completely forget what they've set out to do mid-task, or forget key routine tasks, such as keeping set appointments or caring for their pet.

- Problems with abstract thinking: May have trouble with simple mathematical calculations such as balancing a checkbook or remembering a familiar, often-used phone number.

- Misplacing things: May put things in inappropriate places, such as putting their keys in the microwave, toothbrush in the kitchen cabinet, or their briefcase in the refrigerator.

- Repeated and sudden changes in mood and behavior: May begin exhibiting out-of-character rapid mood swings for no apparent reason.

- Changes in personality: May start to act in ways that are counter to their usual personality style, for example, acting suspicious, fearful, or confused.

- Loss of initiative to do things: May become passive, unresponsive, express little interest in previously enjoyed activities and require real encouragement to get involved.

Studies indicate that as many as one in ten cases of dementia-like symptoms may actually be caused by something less serious and more reversible, such as medication or depression.

While American adults fear Alzheimer's disease more than heart disease, stroke or diabetes, nearly nine out of 10 have taken no steps to prepare for it. In fact, more than a third have a family member or friend suffering from Alzheimer's and three out of five are concerned that they may someday have to provide for or care for someone with the mind-robbing disease.

People with Alzheimer's Disease can live for another ten or even twenty years after onset. Early diagnosis can make it easier for both sufferers and their families to weigh their options early on and to prepare for the changes that come as the disease progresses. But most important is learning to see the disease for what it is, changing your expectations of what someone with Alzheimer's will be like, and remembering that this can take time.

•

WITH AGE COME THE INNER,
THE HIGHER LIFE. WHO WOULD
BE FOREVER YOUNG, TO DWELL
ALWAYS IN EXTERNALS?
— Elizabeth Cady Stanton

AUTHOR

Paul J. Stano is a member of the American, Ohio, Cleveland, and Parma Bar Associations. He is also a member of the National Academy of Elder Law Attorneys. He has been practicing in the area of Estate Planning since 1982 and in Elder Law since 1990.

Mr. Stano is a second generation advocate for the older American. He is the son of former State Senator Jerome P. Stano who was the co-sponsor of the Homestead Exemption Act and Chairman of the Nursing Home Commission, which monitors and supervises nursing homes in Ohio for compliance with state regulations.

•

AGE IS NOT A PARTICULARLY
INTERESTING SUBJECT. ANYONE
CAN GET OLD. ALL YOU HAVE TO
DO IS LIVE LONG ENOUGH.
— GROUCHO MARX

May every sunrise hold
more promise.

Paul J. Stano